SECOND EDITION

David Nunan

THOMSON

™

HEINLE

United States • Australia • Canada • Mexico • Singapore • Spain • United Kingdom

THOMSON
HEINLE

Go for it!, Second Edition
Student Book 1
David Nunan

Publisher, Global ELT: Christopher Wenger
Editorial Manager: Berta de Llano
Development Editors: Margarita Matte, Ivor Williams
Contributing Writers: Kristin Johannsen, Jeremy Taylor
Director of Marketing, ESL/ELT: Amy Mabley
International Marketing Manager: Eric Bredenberg
Senior Production Editor: Sally Cogliano
Sr. Print Buyer: Mary Beth Hennebury

Project Manager: Kris Swanson
Interior Design/Composition: Miguel Angel Contreras Pérez; Israel Muñoz Olmos
Illustrator: Iñaki (Ignacio Ochoa Bilbao)
Photo Manager: Sheri Blaney
Photo Researcher: Christine Micek
Cover Designer: Linda Beaupre
Printer: Transcontinental Printing

For permission to use material from this text or product, submit a request online at: www.thomsonrights.com.
Any additional questions about permissions can be submitted by email to thomsonrights@thomson.com.

ISBN: 0-8384-0494-4

Photo Credits:
2: TL: Barbara Stitzer/Photo Edit;TC: Andy Sacks/Getty Images; TR: Michael Newman/Photo Edit; BL: Michael Newman/Photo Edit; 4: Vicky Kasala/Getty Images; 5: L: Helen King/CORBIS; R: Jeff Greenberg/Photo Edit; 6: Diaphor Agency/Index Stock Imagery; 8: all: Hemera Photo Objects; 13: Hemera Photo Objects; 14: SW Production/Index Stock Imagery; 19: TL: Lawrence Manning/CORBIS; TR: Stockbyte/Superstock; CL: Carolyn Ross/Index Stock Imagery; CR: Frank Simonetti/Index Stock Imagery; BL: SW Production/Index Stock Imagery; BR: Hemera Photo Objects; 20: Hemera Photo Objects; 22: all: Hemera Photo Objects; 24: Michael Newman/Photo Edit; 25: Digital Vision/Getty Images; 31: Table Mesa Prod./Index Stock Imagery; 33: L: Heinle; C: Table Mesa Prod./Index Stock Imagery; R: Heinle; 36: David Young-Wolff/Photo Edit; 39: L, all, Hemera Photo Objects; R, DiMaggio/Kalish/CORBIS; 41: Table Mesa Prod./Index Stock Imagery; 45: TR: Hemera Photo Objects; TL: Howard Sokol/Index Stock Imagery; CR: Hemera Photo Objects; BL: Hemera Photo Objects; BR: Omni Photo Communications Inc../Index Stock Imagery; 47: T: Hemera Photo Objects; B: Omni Photo Communications Inc./Index Stock Imagery; 52: TL: Kwane Zikomo/Superstock; TC: Lisa Peardon/Getty Images; TR: Bob Krist/CORBIS; BL: Spencer Grant/Photo Edit; BC: HIRB/Index Stock Imagery; BR: Richard Hutchings/Photo Edit; 58: L: Peter Johnson/CORBIS; R: Reuters New Media Inc./CORBIS; 59: Bettmann/CORBIS; 61: Pete Saloutos/CORBIS; 62: both, Bettmann/CORBIS; 64: L: Richard Hutchings/Photo Edit; R: David Joel/Getty Images; 69: L: Reuters New Media Inc./CORBIS; R: Bettmann/CORBIS; 72: Roy McMahon/CORBIS; 73: HIRB/Index Stock Imagery; 75: Spencer Grant/Photo Edit; 76: Will Hart/Photo Edit; 79: Michael Newman/Photo Edit; 80: Patrik Giardino/COR-BIS; 81: Michael Wolf/Aurora Photos; 86: TR: Michele Burgess/Index Stock Imagery; BL: Hemera Photo Objects; BC: Hemera Photo Objects; BR: Shirley Vanderbilt/Index Stock Imagery; 87: L: AFP/CORBIS; C: Rufus F. Folkks/CORBIS; R: Rufus F. Folkks/CORBIS; 90: Allana Wesley White/CORBIS; 93: Image Source Limited/Index Stock Imagery; 94: T l to r: Heinle; Doug Mazell/Index Stock Imagery; Tom Holton/Superstock; Doug Mazell/Index Stock Imagery; B l to r: SW Production/ Index Stock Imagery; bottom second from left: Benelux Press/Index Stock Imagery; bottom second from right: Jose Luis Pelaez, Inc./COR-BIS; BR, G.D.T./Getty Images; 95: T: RF/CORBIS; B l to r: Stewart Cohen/Index Stock Imagery; Fotopic/Index Stock Imagery;Paul Viant/Getty Images; RF/CORBIS; 101: Heinle; 103: Image Source/Superstock; 107: TL: Superstock; BR: RF/COR-BIS; 108: T l to r: Karen Huntt Mason/CORBIS, Hulton-Deutsch Collection/CORBIS, RF/Corbis, John Warden/Index Stock Imagery; MT l to r: Gallo Images/CORBIS; Steve Bloom/Getty Images; MB l to r: Ernest Manewal/Superstock, Keren Su/COR-BIS, Zefa Visual Media - Germany / Index Stock Imagery; B l to r: Alan Briere/Superstock, Gary Vestal/Index Stock Imagery; Lynn Stone/Index Stock Imagery; 109: T: Bill Bachmann/ Index Stock Imagery; B: Hemera Photo Objects; 110: Stephanie Maze/COR-BIS; 112: T: RF/CORBIS; M: Karen Huntt Mason/CORBIS; B: RF/CORBIS; 120, L: Alyx Kellington/Index Stock Imagery; M: Bill Lai/Index Stock Imagery; R: Jenni Woodcock; Reflections Photolibrary/CORBIS; 121: L: Jim Cummins/CORBIS; M: Hemera Photo Objects; R: Arthur Beck/CORBIS; 122: L: Bettmann/CORBIS; R: GOLDEN HARVEST/ PARAGON/ THE KOBAL COLLECTION/ LAM, ROBERT; 123: L to r: Hemera Photo Objects, Hemera Photo Objects, Shirley Vanderbilt/Index Stock Imagery, Michelle Burgess/Index Stock Imagery

Acknowledgments

The author and publisher would like to thank the following individuals who offered many helpful insights, ideas, and suggestions for change during this revision of **Go for it!**

- Vera André de Almeida, IBEU, Brazil

- Athiná Arcadinos Leite, ACBEU-Salvador-Bahia, Brazil

- William Bagnall, Toin Gakuen High School, Japan

- Tiffany Chang, Li-Ming High School, Taiwan

- Karen Cronin, Seigakuin Senior High School, Japan

- Correy Day, Swaton Language Institute, Korea

- Walkiria Darahen, ACBEU-Ribeirão Preto, CCBEU-Tupã, Brazil

- Jaime Félix, Centro de Idiomas, Universidad Autónoma de Sinaloa (PISI Guasave), Mexico

- Vivian Rosio Figueredo, Colegio Magister/Colegio Pequenoposlis, Brazil

- Ann Flannigan, Ritsumeikan High School, Japan

- James Gratziani, Toin Gakuen High School, Japan

- Lindsay Huang, C.K. Vocational School, Taiwan

- Sonia Izquierdo Candiotti, Colegio Part "María Auxiliadora", Peru

- Hyo-Soon Kim, Yoo-Suck Elementary School, Korea

- Mei-Hua Lan, Tzu-Hui Institute of Technology, Taiwan

- Mirian Nitzoff, Alianza Cultural Uruguay Estados Unidos de América, Uruguay

- Paula Pacheco Costa Reis, Casa Thomas Jefferson, Brazil

- Marcília da Penha Taveira, Casa Thomas Jefferson, Brazil

- Donovan Ramage, St. Francis High School, Taiwan

- Colleen Ryan, Yokohama Eiwa Girls' Junior and Senior High School, Japan

- Dora Sajevicius, Alianza Cultural Uruguay Estados Unidos de América, Uruguay

- Leah Ann Sullivan, Trident College of Languages, Japan

- Hank Timmers, Kumon International Gakuen Junior High School, Japan

- Russel Tennant, Kumon International Gakuen Junior High School, Japan

- Kai-Ping Wang, Ta-Zen Institute of Technology, Taiwan

- Lilian Vaisman, ICBEU-RJ, Brazil

- Ellen Webber, Ritsumeikan High School, Japan

- Trudi Wimberley, Trident College of Languages, Japan

- Hirokazu Yamanaka, Kansai Soka High School, Japan

- Han Ji Yeon, Ewha Institute, Korea

Book 1: Contents

Unit	Goals	Language	Structures	Vocabulary
13 Around the world page 85	Ask where people are from and what languages they speak	Where's your e-pal from? What languages do you speak?	*Where* questions with *from* and *live*	Countries languages nationalities
14 Everyday activities page 91	Talk about what people are doing	What are you doing? I'm doing my homework.	Present progressive *what* questions *yes / no* questions	Action verbs locations
Language review 7 page 97				
15 Around town page 99	Ask about and say where things are located	Where's the food court? Is there a park in your neighborhood?	Prepositions of place: *between, across from, next to*	Places
16 Animals page 105	Give reasons describe animals	Why do you like snakes? I think dolphins are friendly.	*Why* questions *because* adverbs: *very, really, kind of*	Animals adjectives habitats
Language review 8 page 111				

ACTIVITY ICONS

Listening

Pairwork, class activity

Reading

Writing

Language you can use in the classroom!

Open your books to page (number).

Close your book.

Work with a **partner**.

Work in **groups**.

Ask and **answer**.

Listen and **repeat**.

Write your name.

Circle the answer.

Unit 1

LESSON A
My name's Gina.

1 Warm up

CD1 T-2

a Listen and number the conversations 1 to 3 in the picture.

b Practice the conversations in the picture.

C Now meet other students in the class.

A: What's your name?

B: My name's _____. What's your name?

A: My name's _____.

2 Listen in

CD1
T-3

a Listen to the three conversations, and number the pictures 1 to 3.

CD1
T-4

b Listen again, and complete the conversations with the words from the box.

is	your	I'm	Our	name's
his	name's	name	your	

Conversation 1

Tony: Hello. What's _____ name?

Jenny: My _____ Jenny.

Tony: _____ Tony.

Jenny: Nice to meet you, Tony.

Conversation 2

Bill: What's _____ name?

Maria: His _____ Tony.

Bill: And what's her_____?

Maria: Her name _____ Jenny.

Conversation 3

Teacher: What are _____ names?

Jerry: _____ names are Jerry and Sam.

Sam: I'm Sam, and he's Jerry.

Teacher: Welcome to the class.

c Practice conversation 1 with a partner. Then talk about yourself.

3 Grammar focus

a Study the questions and answers in the box.

Questions	Affirmative answers	
What's your name?	I'm Jenny.	My name's Jenny.
What's his name?	He's Tony.	His name's Tony.
What's her name?	She's Gina.	Her name's Gina.
What are your names?	We're Ben and Mark.	Our names are Ben and Mark.
What are their names?	They're Bill and Naoki.	Their names are Bill and Naoki.

b Complete the questions and answers.

1. What's your name? _____ name's Billy.
2. What's _____ name? His name's Tom.
3. What are your names? _____ names are Anna and Kate.
4. What are their names? _____ names are Greg and Alicia.

c Ask a few of your classmates their first names and last names. Make a list. Then ask about other students in the class.

First name	Last name
Grace	Wong

What's her first name?

Her first name's Grace.

4 Get it together

Play the name game.

My name is Tony.

His name is Tony.
My name is Miki.

His name is Tony.
Her name is Miki.
My name is Ben.

LESSON B What's your phone number?

1 Talk about it

a Listen and repeat.

CD1 T-5

0 "oh"	5 five
1 one	6 six
2 two	7 seven
3 three	8 eight
4 four	9 nine

b Listen and match the names and telephone numbers. Then listen again and complete the telephone numbers.

CD1 T-6

1. Alfonso	c	a. 929-31_____ _____
2. Rita		b. 398-61_____ _____
3. James		c. 278-79_____ _____
4. Mary		d. 555-80_____ _____

c Ask four class members their names and phone numbers and fill in the address book.

NAME: _____   PHONE NUMBER
_____   _____

NAME: _____   PHONE NUMBER
_____   _____

NAME: _____   PHONE NUMBER
_____   _____

NAME: _____   PHONE NUMBER
_____   _____

d Tell the class about yourself and a friend.

My name is Lillian. My phone number is 378-6543. My friend is Kim. Her phone number is 281-9176.

What's your phone number, Kim?

It's 281-9176.

2 Reading

a Find six first names and one last name in the unit. Write them in the correct column.

First name	Last name

b Read the following e-mail messages. (Circle) the first names. Underline the last names.

Hi Molly,

My name is Maria Suarez. I am your new e-pal. These are my sisters. Their names are Conchita and Miriam.

Please write to me soon and send me some photos of your family.

Maria

Dear Mike,

Here is a picture of my best friends. Their names are Benny Chase and Peter Tan.

Best wishes,
Simon Ingram

c Read the e-mails again, and complete the following statements.

1. Molly and _____ are e-pals.
2. Conchita, Miriam, and _____ are sisters.
3. Simon's friends are _____ and _____ .
4. Simon's e-pal is _____ .

3 Writing

a Look at the ID card for Tanya and complete her sentences.

Riverside Middle School

First name: Tanya
Last name: Lopez
Telephone number: 535-2375

My name is _____ .
My telephone number is _____ .

b Fill in your own ID card, and then write about yourself.

First name: _____
Last name: _____
Telephone number: _____
_____

4 Go for it!

Write your phone number on a piece of paper and put it in a bag. Then take another piece of paper out of the bag and find the owner.

What's your phone number?

It's 587-6275.

This is your number!

1 2 3

Unit 2

LESSON A
Is that your ruler?

1 Warm up

CD1
T-7

a Match the words with the things in the picture. Listen and check your answers.

1. pencil ___h___

2. pen _____

3. book _____

4. eraser _____

5. ruler _____

6. pencil case _____

7. backpack _____

8. calculator _____

9. desk _____

10. notebook _____

CD1
T-8

b Listen and number the conversations in the picture 1 to 3.

C Practice the conversations above. Then talk about your things.

A: Is this your _____?

B: Yes, it is. / No, it isn't.

2 Listen in

 **a** Listen and number the things you hear 1 to 5.

CD1
T-9

☐ ☐ ☐ ☐

 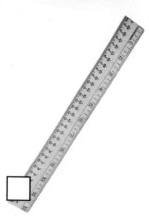  

☐ ☐ ☐ ☐

b Listen again and write the numbers of the items next to their owners.

CD1
T-10 Sam: _____   Tory: _____   Joe: _____   Sonia: _____

c Ask and answer questions about the things in the pictures.

 What's this?  It's a backpack.

d Listen and repeat the alphabet. Then ask how to spell these things.

CD1
T-11

Aa Bb Cc Dd Ee Ff Gg Hh Ii
Jj Kk Ll Mm Nn Oo Pp Qq Rr
Ss Tt Uu Vv Ww Xx Yy Zz

A: How do you spell backpack?

B: B-A-C-K-P-A-C-K

---

8   UNIT 2

3 Grammar focus

a Study the questions and answers in the box.

Questions	Affirmative answers	Negative answers
Is this my pen?	Yes, it is.	No, it isn't. It's his.
Is that Joe's calculator?	Yes, it is.	No, it isn't. It's Susan's.
Are these your pencils?	Yes, they are.	No, they aren't. They're yours.
Are those his books?	Yes, they are.	No, they aren't. They're mine.

LOOK!
This is my notebook.
These are my pencils.

LOOK!
That's my calculator.
Those are my pens.

b Write the words in the correct box.

that   these   this   those

singular (one)

plural (more than one)

c Look at the pictures on page 8 and answer these questions.

1. Is this Sam's backpack? _____

2. Is this Sam's calculator? _____

3. Are these Joe's pencils? _____

4. Is this Tory's eraser? _____

5. Is this Sonia's ruler? _____

4 Get it together

Put objects on the teacher's desk. Ask questions to find the owner of each object.

A: Is this your _____?

B: No, it isn't.

LESSON B Lost and found

1 Talk about it

a Match the words with the things in the picture.

1. cell phone   _a_
2. watch   _____
3. computer disk _____
4. ID card   _____
5. keys   _____
6. English book _____
7. ring   _____
8. wallet   _____

b Listen and (circle) the things that you hear in the box above. Listen again, and write the things in the correct column.

CD1
T-12

Kelsey	Mike

c Fill in the blanks, and then practice the conversation.

Mike: Is that your _____?

Kelsey: Yes, it _____. Great! And look, that's my _____. Hey, Mike, is that _____ cell phone?

Mike: No, it _____.

Kelsey: Is that your _____?

Mike: Yes, _____ is.

d Ask your partner about other items in the Lost and Found.

A: Is that your _____?

B: Yes, it is. Is that your _____?

A: No, it isn't.

---

10   UNIT 2

2 Reading

a Make a list of five things students can lose.

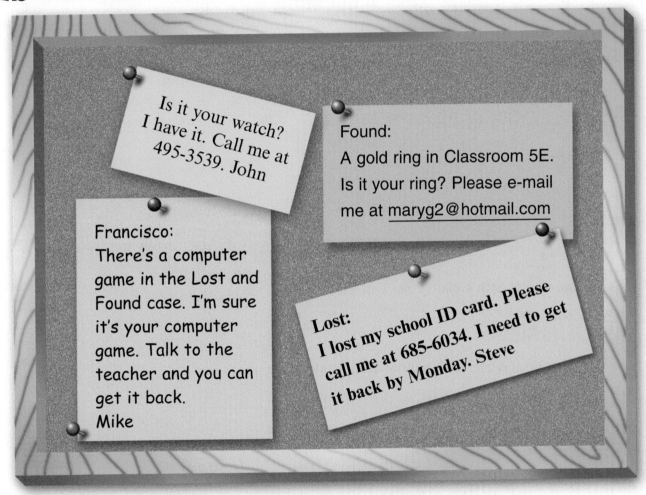

b Read the bulletin board notices, and (circle) the lost items.

Is it your watch? I have it. Call me at 495-3539. John

Found:
A gold ring in Classroom 5E. Is it your ring? Please e-mail me at maryg2@hotmail.com

Francisco:
There's a computer game in the Lost and Found case. I'm sure it's your computer game. Talk to the teacher and you can get it back.
Mike

Lost:
I lost my school ID card. Please call me at 685-6034. I need to get it back by Monday. Steve

c Read the notices again and check ✔ the Lost or the Found column.

Item	Lost	Found
watch		
computer game		
gold ring		
ID card		

3 Writing

a Unscramble these words to make up a lost and found message.

me	Karen	are	Suarez	call	at	keys	your
keys	set	a	of	found	these	284-5348	

b Read the two bulletin board messages. Then write your own lost notice. Include your name and phone number.

Lost
My notebook
My name is Josh.
Please call me: 679-8871.

Lost

Found

Found
One notebook
Is this your notebook?
Call Janna at 679-0442.

c Exchange books with a classmate and write a found message for their notice.

4 Go for it!

Draw a picture on the board. The other students guess what it is.

What's this?

Is it a watch?

Language review 1

a Write the phone numbers.

1. 782-3549: seven

2. 532-0601: _____

3. your phone number: _____ - _____ : _____

4. your friend's phone number: _____ - _____ : _____

b Complete with my, your, his, or her.

1. Hello! _____ name is Amy.

2. Gina is in class 9C. This is _____ classroom.

3. Hello. What's _____ name?

4. That's Tony. _____ last name is Smith.

5. What's _____ phone number, Kenji?

c What's in Susan's backpack? Unscramble the words.

1. rreesa   _____

2. lecl hnope   _____

3. lelwat   _____

4. elurr   _____

5. kotonobe   _____

6. eksy   _____

7. reputomc sidk   _____

8. atmh kobo   _____

9. torcluacla   _____

10. clenpi ecsa   _____

d Unscramble these words to make sentences.

1. name My is Anderson last   _____.

2. books Are Joe's those   _____?

3. that your backpack Is   _____?

4. are names their What   _____?

5. spell you How that do   _____?

13

e Write **this, that, these,** or **those.**

1. _____ pencils
2. _____ computer disks
3. _____ backpack
4. _____ books
5. _____ calculator
6. _____ notebook
7. _____ keys
8. _____ watch

f Write complete answers. ✓ = yes ✗ = no

1. Is that your backpack?
✓ _____

2. Are these your notebooks?
✗ _____

3. Are those Jim's books?
✓ _____

4. Is this Rika's wallet?
✗ _____

Learning log

Write ten useful words you learned
in Units 1 and 2.

1. _____
2. _____
3. _____
4. _____
5. _____
6. _____
7. _____
8. _____
9. _____
10. _____

I can:	Yes	Need more practice
use **my, your, his, her**	☐	☐
use **this, that, these, those**	☐	☐
say telephone numbers	☐	☐
spell words	☐	☐
introduce myself	☐	☐
greet people	☐	☐
identify ownership	☐	☐

Unit 3

LESSON A
Nice to meet you.

1 Warm up

CD1
T-13

a Match the words to the family members in the pictures. Listen and check your answers.

1. cousin _____c_____

2. father _____

3. parents _____

4. brothers _____

5. grandmother _____

6. grandfather _____

7. friend _____

8. grandparents _____

9. (sister) _____

10. mother _____

CD1
T-14

b Listen and look at the word list above. (Circle) the family members you hear.

Is that your sister?

No, it isn't. It's my cousin.

Are those your brothers?

Yes, they are.

c Practice the conversation. Then practice again talking about other family members in the photos.

A: Is that your _____?

B: No, it isn't. It's my _____.

A: Are those your _____?

B: Yes, they are.

2 Listen in

a Listen and (circle) the words you hear.

CD1
T-15

| mother | father | sister | brother | grandmother | grandfather | friend | grandparents |

b Listen and number the people in the order that Hideki meets them. Then write the family names below.

CD1
names below.

T-16

1. _____
2. _____
3. _____
4. _____
5. _____

c You are Dave. Your partner is Hideki. Dave, introduce your family. Then change roles, and practice again.

A: This is my grandfather.

B: Nice to meet you.

C: Nice to meet you, too.

3 Grammar focus

 Study the questions and answers in the box.

Questions	Answers
Is this your grandfather?	Yes, it is.
Is that your sister?	No, it isn't. It's my friend.
Are these your parents?	Yes, they are.
Are those your brothers?	No, they aren't. They're my cousins.

Is she your sister?
Yes, **she** is.

Is he your grandfather?
No, **he** isn't.

Are you Anna's parents?
Yes, **we** are.

Are you Michael's brother?
Yes, **I** am.

 Fill in the blanks in the conversations, and then practice them.

A: Is that your sister?

B: Yes, —————— ——————— . Her name——————— Anna.

A: Are those —————— parents?

B: Yes, —————— ——————— .

A: That's Paul.

B: —————— he your brother?

A: No, —————— ——————— . He —————— my cousin.

Write the name of a family member or a friend on the board. Students guess who it is.

4 Get it together

Scramble one of the words in the box. Then write your scramble on the board. Students will guess the word.

mother   father   sister   brother
parents   grandmother   grandfather
friend   grandparents

LESSON B This is my family.

1 Talk about it

CD1
T-17

a Listen and check ✓ the words you hear.

friend ☐   cousin(s) ☐   dad ☐

mom ☐   twin(s) ☐   grandmother ☐

uncle ☐   aunt ☐   brother ☐   sister ☐

Look!

singular (one)	plural (more than one)
mother	parents
father	
grandmother	grandparents
grandfather	
cousin	cousins

b Write the names of family members on the picture. Ask and answer questions about your family.

A: What's your _____'s name?

B: _____ name is _____ .

This is my family.
These are my parents. These are my
_____ .

c Draw a picture of your family and friends. Now tell your partner about them. Change partners. Ask about your new partner's picture.

Is that your _____?

Yes, it is.

What's _____ name?

_____ .

2 Reading

a Find eight family words in the unit. Write them in the correct columns.

Male	Female

b Read the Web page. (Circle) the family words.

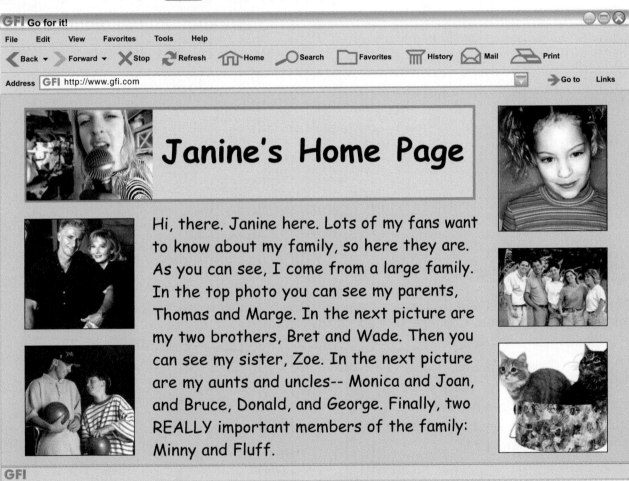

GFI Go for it!

File   Edit   View   Favorites   Tools   Help

Back ▾   Forward ▾   ✕ Stop   ↻ Refresh   🏠 Home   🔍 Search   📁 Favorites   History   ✉ Mail   Print

Address   **GFI** http://www.gfi.com   → Go to   Links

Janine's Home Page

Hi, there. Janine here. Lots of my fans want to know about my family, so here they are. As you can see, I come from a large family. In the top photo you can see my parents, Thomas and Marge. In the next picture are my two brothers, Bret and Wade. Then you can see my sister, Zoe. In the next picture are my aunts and uncles-- Monica and Joan, and Bruce, Donald, and George. Finally, two REALLY important members of the family: Minny and Fluff.

GFI

c Read the Web page again, and complete the following statements.

1. _____ is Janine's sister.

2. Wade is Janine's _____ .

3. Janine's aunts are _____ and _____ .

4. Thomas is Janine's _____ .

5. _____ , _____ , and _____ are Janine's uncles.

6. _____ and _____ are Janine's pet kittens.

3 Writing

a Complete the letter with these words.

brothers   parents   Nicky   family

Dear Teresa,

This is my _____. These are
my _____ and these are my
_____, Tony and Bob. And
this is my sister _____.

Write soon.

Paul

b Bring a photo of your family to class and write a letter about them.

Here is a photo of my family.
These are my parents...

4 Go for it!

Scramble five photos and five letters from exercise **b**. Put them on the board. Take turns matching the photos and letters. Talk about the family.

This is a photo of Helen's family. These are her parents. This is her brother, Jack, and these are her sisters, Anita and Leila.

Unit 4

LESSON A
Where is my backpack?

1 Warm up

CD1 T-18

a Match the words with the pictures. Listen and check your answers.

1. table _e_
2. bed ____
3. game console ____
4. bookcase ____
5. sofa ____
6. chair ____
7. television ____
8. living room ____
9. kitchen ____
10. bedroom ____

CD1 T-19

b Listen and number the things 1 to 4.

Where's my backpack?

It's in the bedroom.

Where are my books?

They're on the sofa.

Where's my game console?

It's under your bed.

c Practice the conversation. Then ask and answer questions about other things in the picture.

A: Where's the _____?

B: It's _____ the _____ .

A: Oh, okay. Thanks.

2 Listen in

a Listen and number the things 1 to 8 in the order that you hear them.

CD1
T-20

b Listen again. Check ✔ the places where the things are.

CD1
T-21

on

in

under

c Practice the conversation. Then ask and answer questions about other things in the picture.

Is the ball on the sofa?

No, it isn't. It's under the chair.

Oh, okay. Thanks a lot.

d Put these sentences in order to make a conversation, and then practice it.

____ I don't know.

_1_ Is the book in the kitchen?

____ No, it isn't.

____ Is it in the bedroom?

3 Grammar focus

a Study the questions and answers in the box.

Questions	Answers
Where's the baseball?	It's in your backpack.
Where's the notebook?	It's under the chair.
Where are your books?	They're on the table.
Where are the pens?	They're on the teacher's desk.

Look!
Is the computer game under the bed?
Yes, it is.
Are the keys on the dresser?
No, they aren't. They're on the table.

Where's = Where is

b Look at the pictures. Complete the conversations and then practice them.

1. A: Where _____ the keys?
   B: They're _____ the dresser.

2. A: Where _____ the game console?
   B: It's _____ the table.

3. A: Where _____ the pencils?
   B: They're _____ the backpack.

4 Get it together

Student A, look at the picture on page 21. Student B, look at the picture below. Talk about where things are in your pictures. Find the differences.

A: Where's the backpack?
   Is it in the bedroom?
B: No, it isn't. It's on the table.

LESSON B Is my math book on the bed?

1 Talk about it

a Match the words with the things in the picture. Listen and check your answers.

CD1
T-22

1. math book _____
2. alarm clock _____
3. sunglasses _____
4. videocassette _____
5. baseball cap _____
6. CD case _____
7. night table _____
8. telephone _____

b Listen and circle the things in the box above that Tommy wants from his room.

CD1
T-23

c Complete the statements. Use this information to practice a conversation between Tommy and his mom.

The math book is _____.

The baseball cap is _____.

The CD case is _____.

The sunglassess are _____.

The videocassette is _____.

Mom: Where's your math book?

Tommy: It's on the night table.

d List two objects in each room. Your partner guesses where something is.

Kitchen	Living room	Bedroom

A: Where's the chair?

B: Is it in the bedroom?

A: No, it isn't!

2 Reading

a Which of these things do you have? Where do you put them?

What?	Yes / No	Where?
computer	yes	on my desk
CD player		
cell phone		
school things		
books and magazines		

 b Read the magazine article, and (circle) the things that May has.

Where do you keep your things?

In many Asian cities, people live in small apartments. Most kids share their bedroom with brothers and sisters, and there is very little space. May Wong lives in Hong Kong. She shares her bedroom with her sister. She keeps her school things — pens, pencils, ruler, eraser — in her backpack, and she keeps her backpack under her bed. She keeps her books in a bookcase. The bookcase is on her desk. She and her sister have a CD player. They keep the CD player on a small table next to May's bed. "I have

a collection of fashion magazines and I keep these in a box under my sister's bed," says May. "There's not much space under my bed!"

c Read the article again and write where May keeps these things.

What?	Where?
school things	
backpack	
books	
fashion magazines	
CD player	

3 Writing

a Complete the e-mail with words from the box. Look for the answers in the picture on page 24.

b Write a note to a friend asking for four things from your room. Say where they are.

sunglasses	baseball cap	math book	CD case
on the bookcase	on the table	on the bed	under the bed

GFI Go for it!

File Edit View Favorites Tools Help

Back ▾ Forward ▾ ✕ Stop ⟳ Refresh 🏠 Home 🔍 Search 📁 Favorites ▥ History ✉ Mail 🖨 Print

Address GFI http://www.heinle.com   ➜ Go to   Links

Message

Accept   Reply   Forward   Delete   Print   Move to

From: _____   Attachments:
To: _____
Copy: _____
Subject: _____

Hi Sally,

Can you bring some things to school? I need my baseball

cap, my math book, my CD case, and my sunglasses. My

baseball cap is _under the bed_ . My _____

is _____ . My _____ is _____

_____ , and my _____

are _____ .

See you,

Tommy

GFI

4 Go for it!

Draw your partner's ideal room. Then describe it to the class.

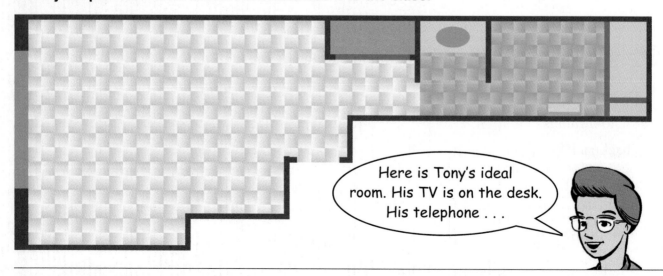

Here is Tony's ideal room. His TV is on the desk. His telephone . . .

Language review 2

a Look at Lisa's family tree. Complete the sentences.

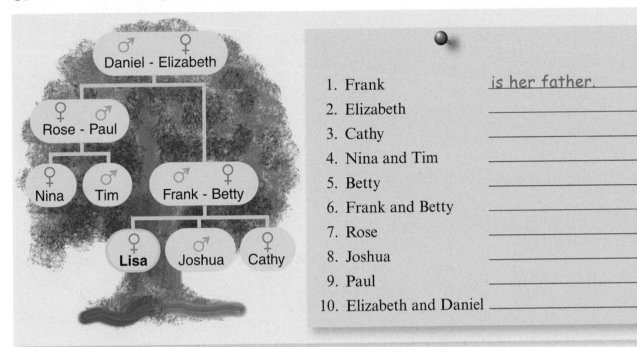

1. Frank   _is her father._
2. Elizabeth   _____
3. Cathy   _____
4. Nina and Tim   _____
5. Betty   _____
6. Frank and Betty   _____
7. Rose   _____
8. Joshua   _____
9. Paul   _____
10. Elizabeth and Daniel   _____

b Complete the conversations.

Are those _____ grandparents?

Yes, _____ _____

That's Sally.

No, _____ _____. _____ my cousin.

_____ she your sister?

c What's in it? Write as many things as you can.

In my kitchen	In my living room	In my bedroom
table		

d Fill in the blanks.

A: Where _____ my books?

B: _____ on your desk.

A: Where _____ my computer game?

B: _____ on the table.

e Unscramble the sentences to make conversations.

1. A: cousin my This is _____ .
   B: you Nice meet to _____ .
   C: Nice too to you meet _____ .

2. A: brothers Are your those _____ ?
   B: are Yes they _____ .

3. A: my glasses the table on Are _____ ?
   B: aren't they No _____ .
   B: desk on the They're _____ .

4. A: books are my Where _____ ?
   B: sofa the They're on _____ .
   A: case about How my pencil _____ ?
   B: your backpack It's in _____ .

Learning log

Write ten useful words you learned in Units 3 and 4.

1. _____
2. _____
3. _____
4. _____
5. _____
6. _____
7. _____
8. _____
9. _____
10. _____

I can:	Yes	Need more practice
talk about my family	☐	☐
introduce people	☐	☐
ask **Where is / are___**?	☐	☐
use **in**, **on**, and **under**	☐	☐

Unit 5

LESSON A
Do you have a baseball?

1 Warm up

CD1
T-24

a Match the words with the objects. Then listen and check your answers.

1. tennis racket _c_
2. baseball bat ___
3. soccer ball ___
4. volleyball ___
5. basketball ___
6. rollerblades ___
7. skateboard ___
8. computer ___
9. comic books ___
10. DVDs ___

CD1
T-25

b Listen. Circle the words you hear.

baseball

basketball

soccer ball

tennis racket

 c Ask and answer questions about the things in the picture. Talk about yourself.

A: Do you have a soccer ball?

B: Yes, I do.

A: Do you have any comic books?

B: No, I don't.

2 Listen in

a Listen and number the conversations 1 or 2. Then listen again and (circle) the answer you hear.

CD1
T-26

___1___ 1. Do you have a tennis racket?   Yes, I do. / (No, I don't.)

_____ 2. Do you have a volleyball?   Yes, I do. / No, I don't.

_____ 3. Does he have a baseball bat?   Yes, he does. / No he doesn't.

_____ 4. Does she have a tennis racket?   Yes, she does. / No, she doesn't.

_____ 5. Does she have a soccer ball?   Yes, she does. / No, she doesn't.

b Listen to Sam and Lucy. Write **S** next to Sam's things and **L** next to Lucy's things.

CD1
T-27

c Listen to the rest of the conversation. What happens? (Circle) the correct answer.

CD1
T-28

Sam and Lucy study math.   Sam and Lucy play tennis.

d Ask and answer the questions at the top of the page. Then talk about yourself.

Do you have a pencil?

Yes, I do.

3 Grammar focus

a Study the questions and answers in the box below.

Questions	Answers	
Do you have rollerblades?	Yes, I do.	No, I don't. I have a skateboard.
	Yes, we do.	No, we don't. We have bicycles.
Does he/she have a baseball?	Yes, he/she does.	No, he/she doesn't. He/She has a tennis ball.
Does it have a famous signature?	Yes, it does.	No, it doesn't. But it has a famous logo.
Do they have a computer?	Yes, they do.	No, they don't. They have a game console.

b Now write these words in the correct box. **I, he, they, you, we, she, it.**

do / don't	
does / doesn't	

don't = do not
doesn't = does not

C Fill in the blanks with **do** or **does**. Practice the conversations.

A: _____ you have a baseball?
B: Yes, I _____.
A: Great! I have a bat. Let's play!

A: _____ Susie have a soccer ball?
B: No, she _____ not.
A: _____ she have a tennis racket?
B: Yes, she _____. I think she has tennis balls too.
A: Hmm… Let's ask.

A: _____ your parents have a computer?
B: Yes, they _____. They have two computers.
A: Well, let's play a computer game.
B: That sounds good.

4 Get it together

Guess what is in your partner's backpack. Make a list. Then ask your partner. You get one point for each correct guess.

a pencil case
an eraser
three pencils
two notebooks

Do you have three pencils?

No, I don't.

LESSON B Let's play computer games!

1 Talk about it

a Match the words and the pictures. Then listen and repeat.

1. interesting __C__   2. boring _____   3. fun _____   4. difficult _____   5. exciting _____

b Listen to Brad and Edgar. What does Brad think about these activities?

Activity	Brad	Edgar
computer games		difficult
volleyball		boring
TV programs		exciting
basketball		fun

Look!

The adjectives don't change.

This is a **great** soccer card collection.
These are **great** soccer cards.
This computer game is **boring**.
I think computer games are **boring**.

c You are Brad and your partner is Edgar.
Use the survey information to make statements.

Edgar thinks computer games are difficult. I think . . .

d Complete the sentences. Then practice making suggestions.

1. Let's play __computer games__ .

2. Let's play _____ .

3. Let's watch _____ .

4. Let's read a _____ .

Let's play computer games.

No, computer games are boring.

32   UNIT 5

2 Reading

 Find the sports words in the unit. Write them in the correct column below.

Things I have	Things I don't have

b Read the school newspaper article. (Circle) the sports words.

9   School News

How do you spend your time?

We asked some students at West Junior High School about activities they do in their free time.

Joey Wilson:
I like to collect things. I have a great soccer card collection. I have 10 cards from Brazil, 5 cards from Japan, and 15 cards from Spain. I trade cards with my friends after school.

Susie Fines:
I think TV and computer games are boring. I like sports. I play volleyball or soccer every Friday at school. I have a new tennis racket, so my new sport is tennis.

Mario Alvarez:
Volleyball is a really interesting game. I play on my school team. It's fun. Sometimes I go to watch international games with my dad. He's a big fan too. I have an autographed volleyball from the Canadian team.

c Read the article again and check ✓ T for true or F for false.

	T	F
1. Susie plays soccer or volleyball every Friday.		
2. Mario plays basketball for his school team.		
3. Joey has soccer cards from China.		
4. Mario's dad likes volleyball.		
5. Joey has 55 cards in his collection.		
6. Joey has cards from Mexico.		

3 Writing

a Write two more questions about sports and games.

Sports and Games Survey

1. Do you have a soccer ball?
   ☐ Yes, I do.   ☐ No, I don't.
2. Do you have a computer game?
   ☐ Yes, I do.   ☐ No, I don't.
3. _____
   _____
4. _____
   _____

b Exchange books with a partner. Answer questions 1 to 4 in the Sports and Games Survey.

c Use the information to write about your partner.

> Tommy has a baseball. He doesn't have a baseball bat.

4 Go for it!

Guess who has it!

Before you play:
1. Write 2 sports objects on pieces of paper.
2. Exchange the papers. Hide them!
3. Choose a *guesser*.
Now: Guess who has it!
You have two chances.

Unit 6

LESSON A
Do you like bananas?

1 Warm up

CD1
T-31

a Match the words with the pictures. Listen and check your answers.

1. hamburger   d
2. tomato   ___
3. broccoli   ___
4. french fries   ___
5. orange   ___
6. ice cream   ___
7. salad   ___
8. bananas   ___
9. sandwich   ___
10. sushi   ___

CD1
T-32

b Listen and number the conversations 1 to 3.

c Practice the conversations. Talk about things in the picture.

A: Do you like salad?

B: No, I don't. How about you?

A: Yes, I do. I love salad.

2 Listen in

a Listen and (circle) the foods you hear.

CD1
T-33

| hamburgers | tomatoes | broccoli | french fries | sushi |
| oranges | ice cream | sandwiches | salad | bananas |

b Listen again to Anna and Yumi. Complete the diagram below.

CD1
T-34

Yumi   Anna

dislikes   dislikes

likes

c Listen to Roberto and Yasmine. Then (circle) the correct answer.

CD1
T-35

1. Yasmine likes _____.

    a. bananas   b. oranges   c. ice cream

2. Roberto likes _____.

    a. bananas   b. oranges   c. ice cream

3. Yasmine and Roberto are _____.

    a. making lunch   b. planning a picnic

d Ask and answer questions about Anna, Yumi, Roberto, and Yasmine. Then ask your partner what he or she likes.

Does Anna like sushi?

No, she doesn't.

Do you like sandwiches?

Yes, I do.

3 Grammar focus

a Study the questions, answers, and statements in the boxes.

Questions	Answers	
Do you like salad?	Yes, I do.	No, I don't.
Do they like oranges?	Yes, they do.	No, they don't.
Does he like sushi?	Yes, he does.	No, he doesn't.

Statements	
I like oranges.	I don't like bananas.
They like salad.	They don't like broccoli.
We like salad.	We don't like french fries.
She likes ice cream.	She doesn't like bananas.

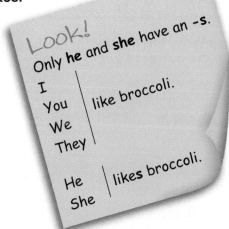

LOOK!
Only **he** and **she** have an -s.

I
You
We   } like broccoli.
They

He
She   } likes broccoli.

b Underline the correct words.

1. I like fruit, but I (don't / doesn't) like vegetables.

2. She (like / likes) salad, but she (doesn't / don't) like sushi.

3. He likes bananas, but he (don't / doesn't) like oranges.

4. We like sandwiches, but we don't (like / likes) french fries.

5. They (likes / like) hamburgers, but they don't like sandwiches.

OPEN

Vegetables   Fruits

C Number these sentences 1 to 6 to unscramble the conversation. Then practice it.

_____ So, let's get sandwiches.

_____ Yes, I do.

_____ Do you like sandwiches?

_____ No, I don't.

_____ Okay.

__1__ Do you like hamburgers?

4 Get it together

Who likes these things. Ask your classmates and write their names next to the food item. The first person to complete the list wins.

A: Rob, do you like ice cream?

B: Yes, I do.

Lesson B I like some fruit, but I hate bananas!

1 Talk about it

a Write the number in the box next to the correct food.

1. broccoli
2. salad
3. eggs
4. apple
5. string beans
6. hamburger
7. watermelon
8. french fries
9. carrots
10. chicken

b Listen and fill in the survey for Katrina and Tom. Then ask and answer questions about what they like and don't like.

CD1
T-36

FOOD SURVEY

	Katrina . . .		Tom . . .	
	likes	doesn't like	likes	doesn't like
Fruit				
apples	☐	☐	☐	☐
oranges	☐	☐	☐	☐
watermelon	☐	☐	☐	☐
Vegetables				
broccoli	☐	☐	☐	☐
carrots	☐	☐	☐	☐
string beans	☐	☐	☐	☐
Other				
eggs	☐	☐	☐	☐
chicken	☐	☐	☐	☐
hamburgers	☐	☐	☐	☐

c Plan a party. Agree on the party foods.

A: Let's get pizza!
B: No, I hate pizza, but I love sushi. Let's get sushi!
A: Okay!

LOOK!
I like ice cream, but I **love** chocolate ice cream!
I don't like vegetables, and I really **hate** broccoli!

2 Reading

a What do you think healthy teenage athletes eat? Check yes, no or maybe.

Food	Yes	Maybe	No
fruit			
vegetables			
chicken			
hamburgers			
potato chips			
ice cream			

 b Read the magazine article. (Circle) the food words.

SPORTS

Runner eats well!

Teenage athlete Katrina Pedrosa is in the news again. The Middlebrook High student is champion runner for the second year. So, how does she do it? "I eat lots of healthy food," says Katrina. "I love fruits and vegetables. For breakfast, I eat a large fruit salad made with apples, bananas, and oranges. Sometimes I like eggs, too. For lunch, I have salad and a sandwich, although on the weekend I like hamburgers and french fries. For dinner, I eat chicken or steak with more salad. And for dessert I have ice cream. I know it's not very healthy, but I love ice cream — especially chocolate!"

 c Read the article again. Answer the questions. Check ✓ T for true or F for false.

	T	F
1. Katrina likes fruit salad.		
2. She eats eggs every day.		
3. She likes chicken for lunch.		
4. She likes hamburgers.		
5. She thinks ice cream is unhealthy.		

3 Writing

a Answer the survey. Then talk with your partner and complete the rest of the survey.

Super Teens and Food				
	I ...		**My partner ...**	
	like	don't like	likes	doesn't like
Breakfast	_____	_____	_____	_____
Lunch	_____	_____	_____	_____
Dinner	_____	_____	_____	_____

A: Do you like _____ for breakfast?

B: No, I don't. I like _____ .

b Write about what you and your partner like for breakfast, lunch, and dinner.

For breakfast, I like _____

For lunch _____

_____

My partner _____ likes _____

_____

_____

4 Go for it!

Work with your partners to make a menu for a class picnic. Share your menu with the class. Vote for the best menu.

Language review 3

a Unscramble the sports words.

1. occres labl _____
2. seabllab tab _____
3. stebbatkall _____
4. lerlolsedbar _____
5. lableylovl _____
6. nesnit tacker _____

b Choose some of the words above and use them in sentences.

You	**Your friend (name: _____)**
1. (skateboard) I don't have a skateboard.	Jose Luis has a skateboard.
2. _____	_____
3. _____	_____
4. _____	_____
5. _____	_____

c Complete the chart.

Do you have . . .	Lucy	Jim and Tim	you
a computer?	yes	no	
a cell phone?	yes	yes	
a tennis racket?	yes	no	
comic books ?	no	yes	

d Now write questions and answers.

1. comic books / Lucy

Does Lucy have any comic books? No, she doesn't.

2. cell phone / you

_____

3. computer / Jim and Tim

_____

4. tennis racket / Lucy

_____

e One word does not belong. Cross it out.

1. oranges   bananas   watermelon   ~~eggs~~
2. carrots   chicken   broccoli   tomatoes
3. pizza   milk   juice   water
4. eggs   chicken   milk   ice cream
5. cake   ice cream   sushi   chocolate
6. dinner   sandwich   lunch   breakfast
7. soda   cake   broccoli   potato chips

f Write sentences about food.

1. Cathy / pizza   😄   Cathy likes pizza._____
2. Kenji / eggs   😄   _____
3. Bill / fruit   ☹   _____
4. Dave and Tom / hamburgers   ☹   _____
5. my friends / sushi   😄   _____
6. I / ice cream   _____
7. I / hamburgers   _____

Learning log

Write ten useful words you learned in Units 5 and 6.

1. _____
2. _____
3. _____
4. _____
5. _____
6. _____
7. _____
8. _____
9. _____
10. _____

I can:	Yes	Need more practice
talk about possessions	☐	☐
ask questions about possessions	☐	☐
talk about food	☐	☐
ask questions about food	☐	☐
make suggestions	☐	☐

Unit 7

LESSON A
How much are these pants?

1 Warm up

CD1
T-37

a Match the words with the things in the picture. Listen and check your answers.

1. socks _____ b

2. T-shirt _____

3. shorts _____

4. sweatshirt _____

5. bag _____

6. sun hat _____

7. pants _____

8. sneakers _____

9. jeans _____

10. swimsuit _____

CD1
T-38

b Circle the words you hear.

sneakers

sun hat

bag

shorts

sweatshirt

How much is this T-shirt?

It's seven dollars.

How much are these socks?

They're two dollars a pair.

 C Practice the conversation below. Then ask and answer questions about other things in the picture.

A: Can I help you?

B: How much is this swimsuit?

A: It's twelve dollars.

B: Thanks.

A: You're welcome.

a Listen and number the things you hear 1 to 5.

CD1
T-39

black   white

red   green

blue   yellow

beige   orange

purple   brown

b Listen again and fill in the blanks.

CD1
T-40

1. The sweatshirts are ____nine____ dollars.
2. Sam likes the _____ sweatshirt.
3. Leila likes the _____ sweatshirt.
4. The bags cost _____ dollars.

5. Leila buys a _____ bag.
6. The shorts are _____ dollars.
7. Sam buys a pair of _____ and a pair of _____ shorts.

C What does one or ones refer to in the sentences below? Write your answers, and then listen again to check.

CD1
T-41

1. I like the blue **one**.   one = ____sweatshirt____
2. The black **one** is really nice.   one = _____
3. I like the yellow **one**.   one = _____
4. Which **ones** do you want?   ones = _____

d Practice the conversation below. Then talk about the things you like, and ask how much they cost.

A: I like the blue sweatshirt. How much is it?

B: It's nine dollars.

3 Grammar focus

a Study the questions and answers in the chart.

Questions	Answers
How much is the red sun hat?	It's eight dollars.
How much is the black one?	It's six dollars.
How much are the black socks?	They're four dollars.
How much are the red ones?	They're three dollars.

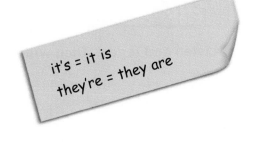

it's = it is
they're = they are

b Write the things in the correct spaces.

T-shirt   bag   sneakers   sun hat   jeans   shorts   sweatshirt

How much is . . . ?	
How much are . . . ?	

c Fill in the blanks. Then practice the conversation.

A: How much _____ the red sun hat?
B: _____ six dollars.

A: How much _____ the blue jeans?
B: _____ nine dollars.

d Now talk about these things.

$6.00
$5.00
$9.00
SALE
$7.00
$8.00

4 Get it together

Student A, look at the things in the photo for a minute; then close your book. Student B, ask questions.

How much are the sunglasses?

Um, they're six dollars.

How much is the wallet?

It's five dollars.

LESSON B The shorts are sixteen dollars.

1 Talk about it

a Listen and repeat. Then write a number next to the number word.

CD1
T-42

| 10 | 11 | 12 | 13 | 14 | 15 | 16 | 17 | 18 | 19 | 20 | 21 | 22 | 23 | 24 |
| 25 | 26 | 27 | 28 | 29 | 30 | 31 | 40 | 50 | 60 | 70 | 80 | 90 | 100 | |

ten _____ ninety _____ fifteen _____ eleven _____ twenty-two _____ sixty _____ twelve _____

fourteen _____ sixteen _____ twenty-five _____ seventy _____ seventeen _____ nineteen _____

twenty _____ twenty-one _____ fifty _____ thirteen _____ twenty-three _____ twenty-four _____

eighteen _____ twenty-six _____ twenty-eight _____ twenty-nine _____ eighty _____ thirty _____

one hundred _____ twenty-seven _____ thirty-one _____ forty _____

b Listen and (circle) the things that Lisa and her mom discuss. Check ✓ the things that Lisa buys.

CD1
T-43

Look!
What does the black swimsuit cost?
It costs forty dollars.
What do the jeans cost?
They cost thirty dollars.

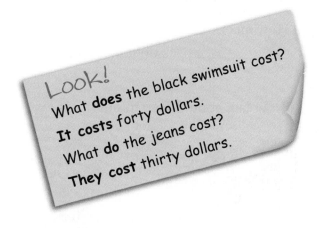

c Practice these conversations.

A: I like the brown hat.
B: What does it cost?
A: Ten dollars.

B: I like the black sneakers.
A: What do they cost?
B: Forty dollars.

d Look at the items listed below and write how much you think they cost. Then ask and answer questions about the items.

$30.00 _____ _____ _____ _____ _____

2 Reading

a Make a list of things that go on sale.

_____

_____

_____

_____

_____

b Read the advertisement and (circle) the things that the shop has on sale.

Blue Water Surf Shop Sale

$25 $12

$30 $14

Yes, folks, it's time for our annual clothing sale. We only have this sale once a year. This year, prices are lower than ever, but the quality of our clothes is the same. How much are our blue jeans? Can you believe they're only twelve dollars? How much are our swimsuits? This week, you can buy one for only fourteen dollars. And what do our T-shirts cost? Only eight dollars each! Or, you can buy two for fifteen dollars. And we have them in a range of colors: red, yellow, blue, and green. Do you like Mango sweatshirts? This week, you can buy them for eighteen dollars. And our sports bags are only twelve dollars — that's right, twelve dollars only.

**Come to the Blue Water Surf Shop now.
The sale starts today.**

c Read the advertisement again, and write the items on sale and the prices.

_____

_____

_____

_____

_____

3 Writing

a Look at the picture. Complete the blanks in the advertisement.

World of Sports
Annual Sale

Don't miss the World of Sports annual sale!

The _____ are only _____ .

How much are the _____ ?

Only _____ .

And the _____ are _____ .

b Write your own advertisement. Follow the model in a.

4 Go for it!

Student A: You want to sell these things. Decide how much you want for each one. Ask how much student B's things cost, and decide what you want to buy.

A: What does the TV cost?

B: It costs $30.

Student B: You want to sell these things. Decide how much you want for each one. Ask how much A's things cost, and decide what you want to buy.

A: How much are the CDs?

B: They're $3 each.

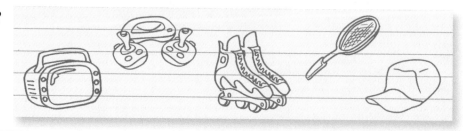

Unit 8

LESSON A
My birthday's in November.

1 Warm up

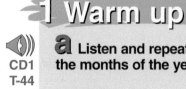

a Listen and repeat the months of the year.

CD1
T-44

1. January
2. February
3. March
4. April
5. May
6. June
7. July
8. August
9. September
10. October
11. November
12. December

 b Listen and match the names and the birthdays.

CD1
T-45

Vera	Jim	Mary	Jennifer	Michael
October 10th	May 15th	August 20th	September 6th	August 5th

C Practice the conversations above. Then ask your classmates about their birthdays.

A: When's your birthday, _____? 	B: When's yours, _____?

B: My birthday is on _____. 	A: Mine is on _____.

2 Listen in

a Listen and repeat.

CD1
T-46

1st	2nd	3rd	4th	5th	6th	7th	8th	9th	10th	11th
12th	13th	14th	15th	16th	17th	18th	19th	20th	21st
22nd	23rd	24th	25th	26th	27th	28th	29th	30th	31st

b Listen and (circle) the numbers you hear above. Then listen again and write the students' names on the class birthday calendar.

CD1
T-47

David

Leila

Nick

Robert

Jane

c Ask and answer questions about your classmates' birthdays.

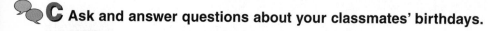

When is Susan's birthday?

Her birthday is on February 14th.

3 Grammar focus

a **Study the questions and answers in the chart.**

Questions	Answers
When's your birthday?	My birthday is on November 11th.
When's his birthday?	Mark's birthday is in August.
When are their birthdays?	Their birthdays are in February.
Is her birthday in June?	Yes, it is.
Is your birthday in December?	No, it isn't. It's on January 3rd.

b **Match the questions and answers.**

Questions	Answers
_____ When's her birthday?	a. No, it's on the 6th.
_____ When are their birthdays?	b. It's in May.
_____ Are their birthdays in October?	c. Yes, it is.
_____ Is his birthday in July?	d. Their birthdays are in June.
_____ Is your birthday on February 5th?	e. No they aren't. They're in November.

c **Fill in the blanks then practice the conversation.**

A: How old are you, Monica?

B: I'm twelve.

A: And _____ your birthday?

B: My birthday is _____ March 12th. How about you and Tommy?

C: Well my _____ is _____ July 5th, and Tommy's birthday is _____ December.

> **LOOK!**
> Sarah has a birthday in September.
> Sarah's birthday is on September 25th.

4 Get it together

Write your birthday on a piece of paper and put it in the teacher's bag. Then take another piece of paper out of the bag and find out who it belongs to.

LESSON B When is the class party?

1 Talk about it

a Match the events with the pictures.

1. __d__ English test
2. ____ party
3. ____ art festival
4. ____ class trip
5. ____ basketball game
6. ____ school play

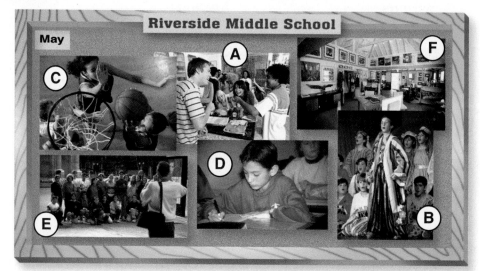

Riverside Middle School

May

b Listen and fill in Joe's calendar.

September	October
24 Sunday _____	1 Sunday _____
25 Monday _____	2 Monday _____
26 Tuesday _____	3 Tuesday _____
27 Wednesday _____	4 Wednesday _____
28 Thursday _____	5 Thursday _____
29 Friday _____	6 Friday _____
30 Saturday _____	7 Saturday _____

C Fill in the blanks and then practice the conversation.

A: Are you going to the _____ ?   A: It's on _____ .

B: When is it?   B: Sounds good.

d Add three more events to the calendar above. Ask and answer questions about your partner's calendar.

A: When's the math test?   B: It's on September 28th.

2 Reading

a Check ✓ the things that happen in your school.

What?	Yes	No
Parents' Day	☐	☐
English-Speaking Day	☐	☐
Art Festival	☐	☐
Music Competition	☐	☐
Student Exchange Day	☐	☐

b Read the school circular. What do the words in **bold** refer to?

we	=	_the school_
you	=	_____
them	=	_____
this day	=	_____
we	=	_____
this	=	_____
this day	=	_____
them	=	_____

Banks High School
"Work hard! Play hard!"

From the Office of the Principal

Dear Students,

Welcome to a new school year. All of us are excited about the things that **we** are doing this term. As **you** know, September is a very busy month. On Monday, September 8th , we have Parents' Day. This is the day for your parents to visit, so don't forget to tell **them**. The Art Festival is on the following weekend, Saturday and Sunday, the 13th and 14th. This is a special event, so please come along. Wednesday the 17th is Foreign Language Day. You can speak any language you like on **this day** — but not English! On September 23rd, **we** have our Music Competition. **This** is your chance to be a star! Finally, September 30th is School Exchange Day. On **this day** we have a visit from Riverside High students. Please help the Riverside students and make **them** welcome.

David James
Principal

c Read the circular again and fill in the table.

What?	When?
Parents' Day	September 8th
_____	_____
_____	_____
_____	_____

3 Writing

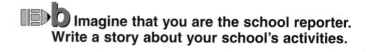

a Make a list of events at your school this month. Then ask questions to find the dates.

WHAT?	WHEN?
English-speaking Competition	February 15th

b Imagine that you are the school reporter. Write a story about your school's activities.

4 Go for it!

Invent a list of five school events and make a calendar. Share your calendars with the class. Vote for the most interesting ideas.

Language review 4

a Label the items.

b Write questions and answers about the picture.

1. A: How _____ socks?
   B: _____ $2.
2. A: How _____ bag?
   B: _____ .

c Put the words in the correct list. Then add two more words to each list.

soccer game	green	March	sweater	school trip	black
birthday	April	blue	swimsuit	May	pants

Colors	Clothing	Month	Event
_____	_____	_____	_____
_____	_____	_____	_____
_____	_____	_____	_____
_____	_____	_____	_____

d Write two things for each color.

1. red   <u>tomatoes</u>   <u>my backpack</u>
2. blue _____ _____
3. green _____ _____
4. yellow _____ _____
5. white _____ _____
6. black _____ _____

e Write the numbers in words. Find the answer.

1. 12 + 20 = ? Twelve plus twenty equals thirty-two.
2. 41 + 16 = ?
3. 75 + 22 = ?
4. 13 + 65 = ?
5. 24 + 50 = ?
6. 81 + 19 = ?

f Unscramble the words for events.

1. shingle etts _____
2. athbirdy trapy _____
3. tra lestivaf _____
4. slacs prit _____
5. llabtekbas mega _____
6. loochs alpy _____

h Complete the conversation.

Anne: _____ your birthday, Bill?

Bill: It's _____ May 10th. How about
your brother? Is _____ birthday _____ May?

Anne: No, _____ _____. His birthday _____
_____ October 3rd.

Learning log

Write ten useful words you learned in
Units 7 and 8.

1. _____
2. _____
3. _____
4. _____
5. _____
6. _____
7. _____
8. _____
9. _____
10. _____

g Write the months in order.

		1	2	3
4	5	6	7	8	9	10
11	12	13	14	15	16	17
18	19	20	21	22	23	24
25	26	27	28	29	30	31

1	2	3	4	5	6	7
8	9	10	11	12	13	14
15	16	17	18	19	20	21
22	23	24	25	26	27	28
29

1	2	3	4	5	6
7	8	9	10	11	12	13
14	15	16	17	18	19	20
21	22	23	24	25	26	27
28	29	30	31

I can: Yes   Need more
                                          practice

talk about possessions   ☐   ☐

ask about prices   ☐   ☐

say dates   ☐   ☐

talk about school events   ☐   ☐

thank someone   ☐   ☐

Unit 9

LESSON A
Do you want to rent a video?

1 Warm up

CD2
T-2

a Listen and repeat the movie types.

1. action movie
2. documentary
3. romantic movie
4. sports video
5. thriller
6. music video
7. comedy
8. drama
9. cartoon
10. sci-fi movie

CD2
T-3

b Listen and (circle) the kinds of videos you hear.

music video

comedy

romantic movie

action movie

documentary

Do you want to rent a video?

Yes, I do. I want to see a music video.

c Practice the conversation. Then make up your own conversation.

A: Do you want to rent a video?

B: Yes, I do. Let's rent a sports video. Do you like sports videos?

A: Yes, I do. / No, I don't.

2 Listen in

a Listen to Ben's and Sally's conversation. Number the kinds of movies in the order that CD2 T-4 you first hear them.

| | action movies | | comedies | | dramas | 1 | music videos | | romantic movies |

b Listen again. On the chart, draw a ☺ under the kinds of movies Ben and Sally like, ☹ under CD2 T-5 the kinds of movies they don't like, and ? for "I don't know."

drama → dramas
comedy → comedies

	action movies	comedies	dramas	music videos	romantic movies
Ben				☹	
Sally					

c Fill in the blanks with words from the conversation. Listen to check your answers.
CD2 T-6

Sally: Let's go to Video World and rent some _____.

Ben: Yeah, that's a good idea.

Sally: Let's rent some _____.

Ben: No. I _____ _____ music videos.

Sally: You don't? So what kinds of things do you like?

Ben: Oh, I like _____ and _____.

d Now practice the conversation. Use information that is true for you.

58   UNIT 9

3 Grammar focus

a Study the questions and answers in the chart.

Look!
I like action movies, **and** I like cartoons.
She likes comedies, **but** she doesn't like dramas.
They like sports videos **and** music videos.

Questions	Answers
Do you want to rent a video?	Yes, I do. / No, I don't.
Does she want to rent a documentary?	Yes, she does. / No, she doesn't.
What kinds of movies do you like?	I like action movies and thrillers.
What kinds of videos does he like?	He likes sports videos, but he doesn't like documentaries.

b Study the sentences in the chart above and complete the sentences below with and or but.

1. I like comedies, _____ I like action movies.

2. Ben likes sci-fi movies, _____ he doesn't like thrillers.

3. Hideki and Maria like music videos, _____ they don't like sports videos.

4. We like thrillers _____ romantic movies.

5. They don't like documentaries much, _____ they like cartoons.

c Fill in the blanks. Practice the conversation.

A: Do you like action movies?

B: _____ don't,

but _____ .

_____ you like?

A: _____ romantic movies

and _____ .

4 Get it together

Find classmates who like the kinds of movies and videos in the chart below. Ask and answer questions to complete the chart.

Find someone who . . .	Student's name
likes comedies and thrillers.	_____
likes action movies, but doesn't like romantic movies.	_____
likes dramas, but doesn't like documentaries.	_____
likes sports videos and cartoons.	_____
likes thrillers and music videos.	_____

LESSON B **Thrillers are scary.**

1 Talk about it

a Study the pictures. Tell your partner the name of a video that each word describes.

scary

funny

silly

sad

spellbinding

fast-moving

b Listen and write **m** for mom or **d** for dad in the appropriate boxes. Then make statements comparing their opinions.

CD2 T-7

Mom thinks _____ are _____ , but dad thinks they're _____ .

	sports	romantic	thrillers
scary			
funny			
boring			
silly			
interesting			

c What do you think? Write a description word for each type of video. Compare your opinions with your partner. Write their description word in the second column.

	Me	Partner 1	Partner 2
comedies			
dramas			
sci-fi movies			
romantic movies			
cartoons			
thrillers			

d Interview another student in the class. Take notes above. Then make statements comparing your partners' opinions.

A: Michael thinks...

2 Reading

 Predict the description words you might read in a review of a movie that you like. (Circle) them.

| great | interesting | boring | funny | exciting | sad | entertaining | scary |

 Read the movie review and <u>underline</u> the description words.

Jackie Rules!

Jackie Tan is a great actor. And he has two new movies. *Kung Fu Charlie* is an action- thriller. It's exciting and scary. His other movie, *Love in Singapore*, is a romance. But it isn't very entertaining. In fact, it's boring. A new actress is also in this movie. Her name is Michele Wong. This is her first movie. She plays a silly girl, but Jackie Tan falls in love with her. The director, Nicholas Tse, wants the movie to be sad. Michele falls in love with someone else! But that happens in lots of movies, doesn't it?

to fall in love

 Read the movie review again. Answer the questions. Check ✓ T for true or F for false.

	T	F
1. Jackie Tan acts in lots of movies.		
2. The writer likes *Kung Fu Charlie*.		
3. Michele acts in lots of movies.		
4. Nicholas Tse is an actor.		
5. The writer likes *Love in Singapore*.		

a Complete the movie review.

_____ is a (n) _____ movie. It stars _____

and _____. They are both _____ actors. I really

_____ this movie.

b Write your own movie review for your school magazine.

Be sure to include:

the name of the movie _____

the type of movie _____

the names of the stars _____

what you think of the movie / the stars _____

_____

_____

4 Go for it!

Play a game with two teams. In turns each team describes a movie but doesn't say the name
of the movie. Students from the other team guess the name of the movie.

This is a romantic movie. It stars Rebecca Thomas and Kirk Farrell. It's very sad.

Is it *Forever Yours*?

Unit 10

LESSON A
Can you play the guitar?

1 Warm up

CD2
T-8

a What can these students do? Match the words and the students. Listen and check your answers.

1. dance _f_

2. swim ___

3. sing ___

4. act ___

5. draw ___

6. speak French ___

7. take photographs ___

8. write stories ___

9. tell jokes ___

10. play chess ___

CD2
T-9

b Listen and number the conversations in the order that you hear them.

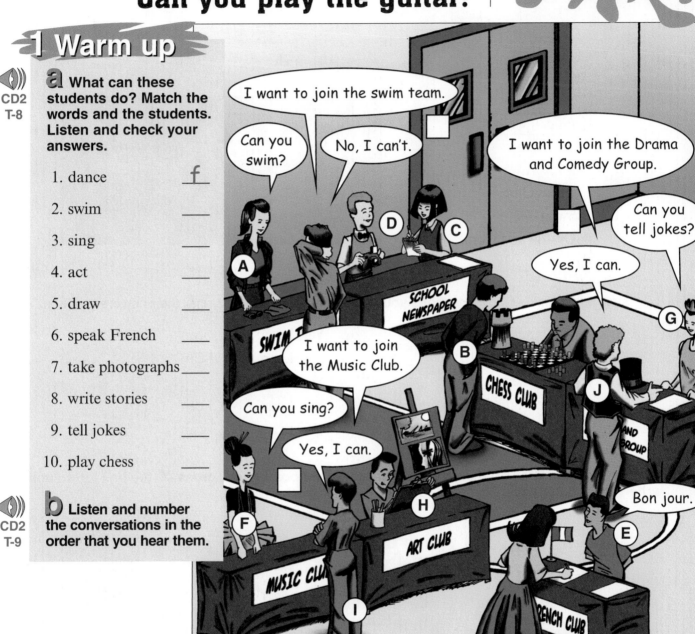

c Practice the conversations in the picture. Then make up your own conversations.

A: I want to join the _____.
B: Can you _____?
A: _____.

2 Listen in

CD2
T-10

a Listen to the conversations, and (circle) the school groups you hear.

® **Riverside High School** **®**

Monday, September 12th

Sign-up Day
School Newspaper
(French Club)
Art Club
Music Club
Chess Club
Swim Team
Drama and Comedy Group

b Listen and check ✓ the questions you hear. Listen again and (circle) the answers you hear.

CD2
T-11

_____ Can you play basketball?   Yes, I can. / No, I can't.

_____ Can you play soccer?   Yes, I can. / No, I can't.

_____ Can you play chess?   Yes, I can. / No, I can't.

_____ Can you play a musical instrument?   Yes, I can. / No, I can't.

_____ Can you sing?   Yes, I can. / No, I can't.

c Can Lucy and Brad do these things? Check ✓ the box for **yes**, cross ✗ the box for **no** and write **?** for "I don't know."

Lucy				
Brad				

d Compare your answers with those of a partner. Ask and answer questions about Lucy and Brad. Then ask your partner what he / she can do.

A: Can Lucy play soccer?   A: Can you play soccer?

B: No, she can't.   B: _____ .

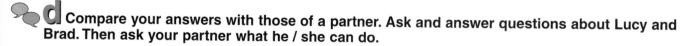

64   UNIT 10

3 Grammar focus

 Study the questions and answers in the chart.

LOOK!
What do you notice?
I **can** swim.
She **can** swim.
We **can** swim.
They **can** swim.

can't = cannot

Questions	Answers
Can you tell jokes?	Yes, I can.
Can she play soccer?	No, she can't, but she can play tennis.
Who can speak Chinese?	Wilson can speak Chinese.
Can they draw?	No, they can't, but they can write stories.

b (Circle) **the correct word. Then ask and answer the questions around the classroom.**

1. Who is / can speak three languages?

2. Who is / can sing?

3. Who is / can thirteen?

4. Who is / can play basketball?

5. Who is / can funny?

Who can swim?

c **Make questions and answers from the words and phrases and then practice them. Example:**

1. Lucia / speak French / speak Spanish

   Can Lucia speak French?
   No, she can't, but she can speak Spanish.

2. Nick / play basketball / play tennis

3. Alana and Jill / act / tell jokes

4. Erik / write stories / take photos

5. Your sisters / dance / sing

6. Nadia / speak Japanese / speak German

4 Get it together

On a piece of paper, write two things that you can do and one thing that you can't do. Take turns telling your classmates that you can do all three things on your list. Mix the order of things you talk about. Your classmates guess which statements are true and which is false.

I can speak German.

No, you can't. I don't believe you!

LESSON B Bill can play the guitar, but he can't sing.

1 Talk about it

a Choose a word that goes with each verb. Write it next to the verb. Then practice using each phrase in a sentence.

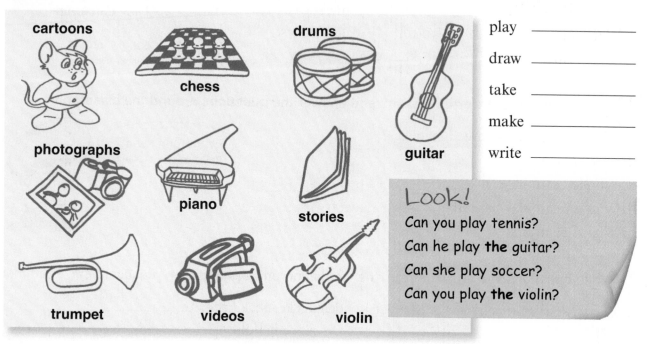

cartoons

chess

drums

photographs

piano

stories

guitar

trumpet   videos   violin

play _____

draw _____

take _____

make _____

write _____

LOOK!

Can you play tennis?

Can he play **the** guitar?

Can she play soccer?

Can you play **the** violin?

b Listen and complete the chart with activities students can and can't do.

CD2
T-12

	can	can't
Bill		
Jennifer		
Victor		

c Talk about what Bill, Jennifer, and Victor can and can't do.

Bill can play the guitar, but he can't sing.

d Plan a Talent Show. Find people who can . . .

	Name
play the guitar	
speak French	
take photographs	
paint	
dance	
sing	
write stories	

2 Reading

a Find all the skills listed in the unit. Write them in the correct column below.

Things I can do	Things I can't do
	-

b Read the advertisements. Match the titles with the advertisements.

☐ Are you looking for a vacation job? Can you clean house and cook? Then I need you. The work is boring, but the pay is good. I need you from 2–5, Monday to Friday. Please call Emily Martin at 293-7742.

☐ Can you speak Spanish? Do you like kids? I need someone to help my daughters learn Spanish during their vacation. It doesn't matter if your Spanish isn't perfect, just as long as you can hold a conversation. Please call Mrs. Johanssen at 555-3721.

☐ Can you play the drums or the guitar? Would you like to make some money this vacation? We need two new band members for our group. Are you interested? Then come for an audition on Saturday afternoon at 2 p.m., Hopewell Center Auditorium.

1 **Musician Wanted**

2 **Conversation Tutor Wanted**

3 **Part-time Cleaning Help**

c Read the advertisements again, and fill in the chart.

Job	Skills

3 Writing

a Fill in the blanks in this advertisement.

Baby-sitter Wanted

_____ you draw and paint? _____ you cook? Can _____ clean up after messy kids? _____ you want to make some pocket money this vacation? We need a baby-sitter for our daughter on Monday and Wednesday evenings. Please e-mail us at nannyforus@aol.com.

b Write an application for the job. Make sure you include the following:

your name

your interests and the things that you can do

your phone number and e-mail address

My name is _____ . I want to be a baby-sitter for your daughter.
I can

4 Go for it!

Imagine that you are a genius with many amazing abilities. Think of five amazing things that you can do. Write them on a piece of paper. Now take turns interviewing other students about their special abilities.

Can you speak Chinese?

Yes, I can. I can speak six languages!

Language review 5

a Unscramble the kinds of movies and videos. Then write a movie title.

1. onocrat   _cartoon_   _Motor Mouse Adventures_ _____

2. marad   _____   _____

3. mentydrocua   _____   _____

4. nicota vieom   _____   _____

5. modyec   _____   _____

6. cramtino emvoi   _____   _____

7. micsu odvie   _____   _____

8. rillther   _____   _____

b Write sentences using these words. Use your own ideas.

1. boring   _Baseball is boring._ _____

2. silly   _____

3. scary   _____

4. interesting   _____

5. funny   _____

6. exciting   _____

c Use and or but to complete sentences 1 through 6. Then make up your own sentences for 7 and 8.

1. I like sports videos, _____ I like thrillers.

2. Jason speaks Spanish, _____ he doesn't speak French.

3. We play tennis, _____ we don't play basketball.

4. I have two brothers, _____ I have one sister.

5. You go to class, _____ you don't study.

6. Susan likes chicken, _____ she doesn't like fish.

7. (Your own idea) _____, and _____.

8. (Your own idea) _____, but _____.

d Complete the chart. Then write questions and answers.

Can . . .	Luis	Aya and Mari	you
speak English?	yes	no	
play tennis?	yes	yes	
sing?	no	yes	

1. (play tennis / Luis) Can _____?

   Yes, _____ .

2. (speak English / Aya and Mari) _____?

   _____ .

3. (sing / Luis) _____?

   _____ .

4. (play tennis / Aya and Mari) _____?

   _____ .

5. (sing / you) _____?

   _____ .

6. (speak English / you) _____?

   _____ .

e Complete each phrase with a word from the box.

Chinese	cartoons	piano	tennis	video	photographs

Learning log

Write ten useful words you learned in Units 9 and 10.

1. _____
2. _____
3. _____
4. _____
5. _____
6. _____
7. _____
8. _____
9. _____
10. _____

1. take _____
2. play the _____
3. play _____
4. speak _____
5. draw _____
6. make a _____

I can:	Yes	Need more practice
describe things with adjectives	☐	☐
give short answers (Yes, I do.)	☐	☐
talk about abilities using **can**	☐	☐
use **and** and **but**	☐	☐

Unit 11

LESSON A

What time do you usually go to school?

1 Warm up

CD2
T-13

a Match the words and the pictures. Listen and check your answers.

1. get up   a
2. get to school   ___
3. run   ___
4. eat breakfast   ___
5. take a shower   ___
6. get dressed   ___
7. brush teeth   ___
8. feed pet   ___
9. leave for school ___
10. go to music lesson ___

b Listen and draw
CD2 lines to match the
T-14 times and actions.

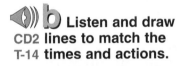

5:00	get to school
6:00	get up
7:00	eat breakfast
8:00	run

c Practice the conversation. Then talk about yourself using other actions in the picture.

A: When do you usually get up?

B: At seven o'clock.

A: And what time do you leave for school?

B: At eight o'clock.

2 Listen in

a Listen to the interview with Rick Starling. Check ✓ the things that Rick talks about.

CD2
T-15

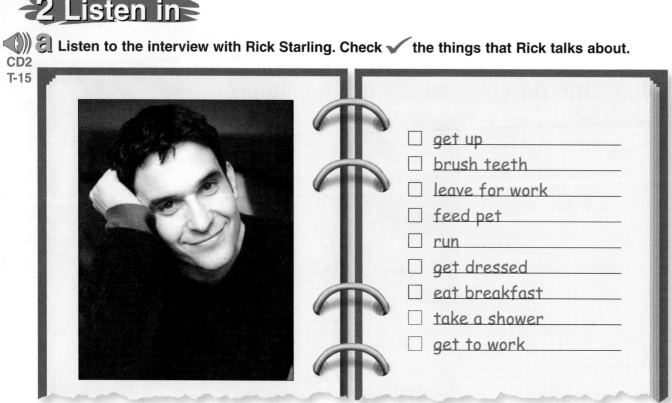

- ☐ get up _____
- ☐ brush teeth _____
- ☐ leave for work _____
- ☐ feed pet _____
- ☐ run _____
- ☐ get dressed _____
- ☐ eat breakfast _____
- ☐ take a shower _____
- ☐ get to work _____

b Listen again and write Rick's activities next to the correct time.

CD2
T-16

05:00
five o'clock _____ get up _____

05:15
five fifteen _____

06:00
six o'clock _____

06:15
six fifteen _____

06:30
six thirty _____

07:00
seven o'clock _____

c Student A is an interviewer. Student B is a celebrity. Ask and answer questions about the celebrity's routine.

A: What time do you _____?

B: I usually _____ at _____ o'clock.

A: What do you do then?

B: I _____.

3 Grammar focus

a Study the questions and answers in the box.

Questions	Answers
What time do you usually get up?	I usually get up at seven o'clock.
What time do they get to school?	They always get to school at eight forty-five.
What time does Rick leave for school?	He leaves for school at eight thirty.
When does Alicia exercise?	She sometimes exercises on Saturdays.
When do you get to school?	I get to school at eight. I'm never late.

b Write the appropriate answers or questions. Use always, usually, sometimes or never. Then practice asking and answering the questions.

1. What time do you get up on school days?

   _____.

2. _____?

   On weekends, I never get up before ten.

3. When do you have breakfast?

   _____.

4. _____?

   I usually run at six o'clock.

5. When do you leave for school?

   _____.

c Write about something you always do, something you usually do, something you sometimes do, and something you never do in your daily life. Then exchange information with another student.

1. I always _____.   3. I sometimes _____.

2. I usually _____.   4. I never _____.

4 Get it together

Interview three of your classmates. Find out what time they do these activities. Then report what you found out to the rest of the class.

	Student 1	Student 2	Student 3
get up on weekends			
run / do exercise			
eat breakfast			
take a shower			
leave for school			
get to school			

LESSON B Healthy living

1 Talk about it

a When do you and your partner do these things? Ask and answer questions to find out.

go to bed	get up
take a shower	brush your teeth
do your homework	do exercise
go to karate class	eat breakfast
eat dinner	

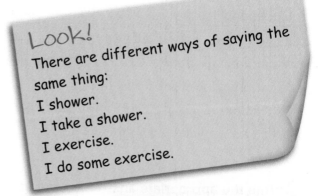

Look!
There are different ways of saying the same thing:
I shower.
I take a shower.
I exercise.
I do some exercise.

in the morning

in the afternoon

in the evening

b Listen and complete the chart with the correct time.

CD2
T-17

	goes to bed	gets up	exercises	eats breakfast	leaves for school
Nina					
Joseph					

c Complete these sentences. Then talk about Nina's and Joseph's schedules.

1. Joseph usually _____ .
2. Nina always _____ .
3. Joseph never _____ .
4. Nina usually _____ .
5. _____ has a healthy lifestyle.
6. _____ has an unhealthy lifestyle.

d Ask and answer questions about your classmates' lifestyles. Are they healthy or unhealthy?

what time you go to bed

what time you get up

when and what you eat for breakfast

when and how you exercise

a Circle the items that you might read about in an article about healthy living.

Eat breakfast every day.

Don't smoke.

Go to a fitness center.

Exercise every day.

b Scan the text. How many tips for healthy living does it contain? Number them.

Tips for Healthy Living

Modern life is very busy. Most of us are very busy every day. Many people rush off to school or work without eating breakfast. This is a mistake. Breakfast is a very important meal. Eat a healthy breakfast every day. Also, it is better to have four or five small meals every day than one or two large meals.

Exercise is also important to staying healthy. Again, it's something that people skip because of lack of time. You don't have to do a lot of exercise.

Experts say that you only need to run or even walk three times every week. This is enough to keep you healthy. Another good thing about exercise is that it makes people feel good.

c What does the article say? Check ✓ the appropriate box.

	Yes	No
1. No one eats breakfast anymore.	☐	☐
2. You should eat four to five meals a day.	☐	☐
3. Exercise makes you happy.	☐	☐
4. You should run every day.	☐	☐

3 Writing

a Number these statements in order to make a passage about a morning routine.

___ I usually go for a run from six thirty to seven o'clock.

___ I always get up at five o'clock and do exercise for half an hour.

___ Then I sometimes go to the school gym at eight o'clock and do aerobics.

___ I love this routine, and I never sleep in, not even on the weekend.

_1_ I have a very healthy morning routine.

b Write about your own morning routine.

4 Go for it!

Work in pairs. Take turns acting out interviews about lifestyles. Ask questions such as, "What time do you go to bed?" and "What time do you get up?" Then decide if the person who was interviewed has a healthy lifestyle or not.

LESSON A
My favorite subject is science.

1 Warm up

CD2
T-18

a Match the school subjects with the pictures. Listen and check your answers.

1. art   _b_
2. history   ___
3. math   ___
4. physical education (P.E.) ___
5. music   ___
6. science   ___
7. French   ___
8. literature   ___
9. geography   ___
10. computer science ___

CD2
T-19

b Listen and (circle) the subjects you hear.

music
history
art
literature
science
math

Midterm Exam Schedule

Grades to be posted over the weekend.

What's your favorite subject?

My favorite subject is science. What's yours?

Midterm Art Projects due on Friday at 12:15 in Room 324.

I like history and geography.

MONDAY:
LITERATURE 10:30,
MUSIC 2:15;
TUESDAY:
P.E. 7:45,
MATH 10:00;
WEDNESDAY:
HISTORY 9:15,
GEOGRAPHY 1:30;
THURSDAY:
FRENCH 8:30,
COMPUTER SCIENCE 11:45;
FRIDAY:
SCIENCE 8:00

Soccer team tryouts this weekend. Saturday 8:00-11:00

c Practice the conversation above. Then make up your own conversation. Give answers that are true for you.

A: What's your favorite subject?   B: What's yours?

B: My favorite subject's _____ .   A: My favorite subject's _____ .

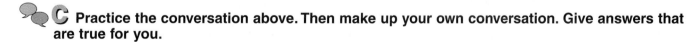

2 Listen in

a Listen and put the conversation in order. Write the letters in the correct speech bubble.

CD2
T-20

a. Because it's fun.

b. My favorite subject is P.E.

c. What's your favorite subject?

d. Why do you like P.E.?

b Listen to Janela, Derek, and Alex. Match the subjects with the descriptive words.

CD2
T-21

physical education (P.E.)   interesting

science   fun

music   boring

art   difficult

drama   cool

math   okay

c Who says what? Listen again, and write **J** for Janela, **D** for Derek, and **A** for Alex.

CD2

T-22 1. _____ Math is boring.

2. _____ My music teacher is nice.

3. _____ My favorite subject is music.

4. _____ P.E. is fun.

5. _____ Math is interesting.

6. _____ Science is okay.

d Complete this conversation, and practice it using information that is true for you.

A: What's your favorite subject?

A: Why do you like _____ ?

B: _____ .

B: Because it's _____ .

3 Grammar focus

a Study the questions and answers in the chart.

Questions	Answers
What's your favorite subject?	My favorite subject's science.
What's her favorite subject?	Her favorite subject's music.
Why do you like history?	Because it's interesting.
Why do Vinnie and Paul hate math?	Because it's difficult.
Why does Janela like Mr. Urbanski?	Because he's great.
Who is your math teacher?	Mrs. Walsh is my math teacher.

b Match the items with the correct question words.

Mrs. Cohen __b__ art ____ because it's interesting ____

geography ____ Mr. Thomas ____ because it's boring ____

a. what   b. who   c. why

c Complete the conversation and then practice it.

A: What _____ _____ favorite subject?

B: My _____ _____ is art.

A: Why _____ you _____ art?

B: Because _____ fun.

A: Who _____ _____ art teacher?

B: Mrs. Mendoza.

d Write questions for these answers.

Questions	Answers
1. _____ ?	Because it's interesting.
2. _____ ?	Science and math.
3. _____ ?	His favorite subject is drama.
4. _____ ?	Because music is cool.
5. _____ ?	Their history teacher is Mr. Wang.

4 Get it together

Ask three classmates questions and complete the chart. Work against the clock. The first student to complete his/her chart is the winner!

Name	Favorite subject What?	Reason Why?	Teacher Who?
Jenny Cliff	computer science	It's fun.	Mr. Boyd

LESSON B Music is cool.

1 Talk about it

a Look at the descriptive words below. Are these words positive (+), negative (-) or neutral (0)? Write the ones you know on the lines.

fun	useful
cool	busy
interesting	challenging
boring	easy
difficult	exciting

positive (+)	negative (-)	neutral (0)

b Listen to Ken describe his week. Confirm or write the descriptive words you hear in the chart above.
CD2 T-23

c Listen again. Circle the classes Ken talks about on his schedule.
CD2 T-24

OCTOBER

Monday 25	Tuesday 26	Wednesday 27
08:00 Study Hall	08:00 Study Hall	08:00 Study Hall
09:00 Computer Science	09:00 Math	09:00 French
10:00 Literature	10:00 Math	10:00 Computer Science
11:00 History	11:00 French	11:00 Geography
12:00 Lunch	12:00 Lunch	12:00 Lunch
13:00 P.E.	13:00 Science	13:00 P.E.
14:00 Geography	14:00 Music	14:00 Literature
15:00	15:00	15:00
16:00	16:00	16:00
17:00	17:00	17:00

Thursday 28	Friday 29	Saturday 30
08:00 Study Hall	08:00	Soccer tryouts
09:00 Math	09:00	
10:00 French	10:00	
11:00 Science	11:00	
12:00 Lunch	12:00	Sunday 31
13:00 History	13:00	
14:00 Geography	14:00	
15:00	15:00	Rent video
16:00	16:00	
17:00	17:00	

NO CLASSES

d Talk about Ken's favorite subject. Then talk about your favorite subject. Why do you like it? When do you have it?

A: What's Ken's favorite subject?

B: _____.

A: Why does he like _____?

B: Because it's _____.

A: When does he have it?

B: On _____ and _____.

> What's your favorite subject?

> History.

2 Reading

a What do you think of these subjects? Write a description word for each one.

Subject	Descriptive word
Math	
Science	
History	
P.E.	
Literature	
Computer Science	
Geography	

b Read the following message. <u>Underline</u> the subjects that Yu Mei likes. (Circle) the subjects she doesn't like. Compare Yu Mei's descriptions with yours above.

Message

| Accept | Reply | Forward | Delete | | Print | | Move to | ▽ |

From: _____   Attachments:
To: _____
Copy: _____
Subject: _____

Hi Jen,
I can't write a lot! Fridays are really busy for me. At 8:00 I have math - ugh! Everyone says it will be useful some day, but I'm not so sure. Then at 9:00 I have science. It's difficult, but interesting. At 10:00 I have history. Boring! But at least I have P.E. to look forward to at 11:00. P.E. is easy and fun. We have lunch from 12:00 to 1:00. The first subject after lunch is literature. It's easy. And I like my literature teacher, Mr. Lopez. He's such fun. My classes finish at 2:00, but after that I have gymnastics club for two hours. This is really challenging! Our teacher is very strict, and we get very tired. And after gymnastics I go to my music club. Music is cool, so that's something else to look forward to.
Your friend,
Yu Mei

GFI

c Complete Yu Mei's schedule with the information in the message.

Friday			
Time	**Subject**	**Time**	**Subject**
8:00 - 9:00	_____	12:00 - 1:00	_____
9:00 - 10:00	_____	1:00 - 2:00	_____
10:00 - 11:00	_____	2:00 - 4:00	_____
11:00 - 12:00	_____	4:00 - 5:00	_____

3 Writing

a Number these sentences in order to make an e-mail.

____ Maybe we can meet tomorrow.		____ Jeff	
____ At five o'clock, I have my Spanish lesson.		____ Thanks for your message.	
____ Then at four o'clock, I have to go to the doctor.		____ At three o'clock, I have my music lesson.	
____ Sorry, but I can't meet you this afternoon.		_1_ Dear Carlos,	

b What's your favorite school day? Make a schedule and then write an e-mail to a friend about it.

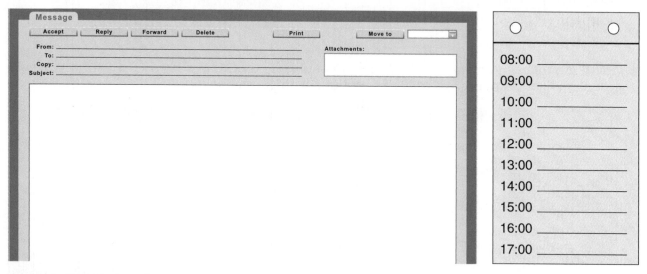

4 Go for it!

Work in groups and make a list of your five favorite subjects, with your favorite in first position. Present your lists to the rest of the class and give reasons for your choices.

Language review 6

a What time is it? Write the answers in words.

1. It's _____ .
2. It's _____ .
3. It's _____ .
4. It's _____ .
5. It's _____ .

① ② ③ ④ ⑤

b Put the words in order to make questions. Then write your answers. Write the times in words.

1. you do get up usually When

_____?

I _____ .

2. do What school time you leave for

_____?

I _____ .

3. When homework you usually do your do

_____?

I _____ .

4. go do bed What to time you

_____?

I _____ .

c Answer the questions. Write sentences with always, usually, sometimes, never.

Do you . . .

1. go to bed at 2:00? _____

2. eat breakfast? _____

3. get up early? _____

4. exercise? _____

5. do your homework? _____

d Write your opinion about the school subjects below. Use these words.

fun	interesting		boring	difficult		cool
useful	dull	hard	challenging	easy		exciting

1. English _I like English because it's useful._
2. _____
3. _____
4. _____
5. _____
6. _____
7. _____
8. _____
9. _____

music	geography
drama	math
science	art
history	p.e.

e Write questions for these answers.

1. _____ ?

Because it's boring.

2. _____ ?

Art and music.

3. _____ ?

Because it's interesting.

4. _____ ?

My favorite subject is drama.

5. _____ ?

Our history teacher is Ms. Park.

Learning log

Write ten useful words you learned in Units 11 and 12.

1. _____
2. _____
3. _____
4. _____
5. _____
6. _____
7. _____
8. _____
9. _____
10. _____

I can:	Yes	Need more practice
say times	☐	☐
talk about schedules	☐	☐
use **always, usually, sometimes, never**	☐	☐
talk about school subjects	☐	☐

LESSON A
Where's your e-pal from?

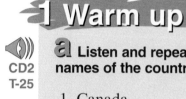
1 Warm up

CD2
T-25

a Listen and repeat the names of the countries.

1. Canada

2. Korea

3. Japan

4. the United States

5. Australia

6. Mexico

7. Brazil

8. Argentina

9. the United Kingdom

10. Turkey

CD2
T-26

b Listen and (circle) the countries above that you hear.

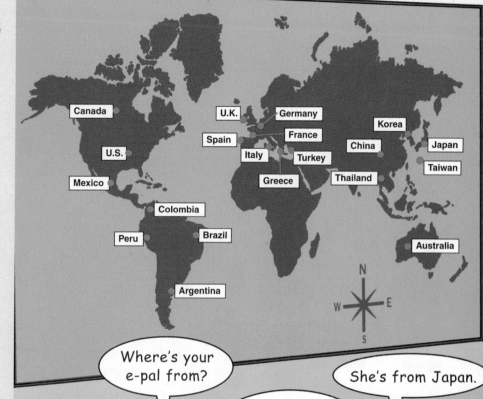

Canada   U.K.   Germany   France   Korea   Spain   China   Japan   U.S.   Italy   Turkey   Taiwan   Mexico   Greece   Thailand   Colombia   Peru   Brazil   Australia   Argentina

N W E S

Where's your e-pal from?

What language do they speak in Japan?

She's from Japan.

They speak Japanese.

c Practice the conversation. Then practice again using other countries on the map.

A: Where's your e-pal from?

B: He's from Turkey.

2 Listen in

CD2
T-27

a Listen to the information about these countries. Match the city, country, and language.

City	Country	Language
Ankara	Australia	Spanish
Lima	Japan	English
Mexico City	Korea	Japanese
Seoul	Mexico	Turkish
Sydney	Peru	Korean
Tokyo	Turkey	Spanish

CD2
T-28

b Listen and fill in the cities and countries you hear.

E-pal's Name	City	Country	Language
Takumi			
Claudia			
Andrew			

c Ask and answer questions about the e-pals in the chart above.

Where does Takumi live?

What language do they speak in Japan?

He lives in Tokyo. It's in Japan.

They speak Japanese.

3 Grammar focus

a Study the questions and answers in the chart.

Questions	Answers
Where's your e-pal from?	He's from Korea.
Where are your friends from?	They're from Canada.
Where do you live?	I live in Huancayo. It's in Peru.
Where does she live?	She lives in Tokyo.

LOOK!

What's his nationality?
He's Japanese.

What languages do they speak
in Hong Kong?
They speak Chinese and English.

b Draw lines to match the questions and answers.

Questions
1. Where's your pen pal from?
2. Where do they speak Turkish?
3. Where are your parents from?
4. What's her nationality?
5. What do they speak in Argentina?

Answers
a. In Turkey.
b. Spanish.
c. She's Korean.
d. They're from Canada.
e. Japan.

c Fill in the blanks and practice the conversation. Then practice again using information that is true for you.

A: What's _____ name?
B: Jose.
A: _____ are you from?
B: Mexico City.

A: _____ your nationality?
B: _____.
A: _____ languages _____ you speak?
B: Spanish _____ English.

4 Get it together

Pretend to be a famous person.
Go around the class and meet
other famous people.

A: What's your name?
B: Russell Crowe.
A: Where are you from?
B: Wellington, New Zealand.

LESSON B What languages do you speak?

1 Talk about it

a Fill in the blanks in the chart. Then talk about the information with your partner.

Country	Nationality	Language
	Egyptian	
	American	
	French	
	Brazilian	
	Argentinean	
	Canadian	

Look!
Japanese, Lebanese
Mexican, Korean
Turkish, English
Australian, Canadian

What do they speak in Egypt?

They speak Arabic.

What's their nationality?

Egyptian.

 b Listen and complete the chart.

CD2
T-29

Name	City	Country	Nationality	Languages
Maria	_____	_____	Mexican	English and Spanish
Simon	Toronto	Canada	_____	_____

 c Take turns as Student A and Student B.
Student A: Choose one of the role cards below. Have a conversation with your partner.
Student B: Talk to Maria or Simon. Ask your partner questions about where he or she is from, his or her nationality, and the languages he or she speaks.

Maria
You are Sophie's e-pal. Talk about yourself.
- where you're from
- your nationality
- what languages you speak

Simon
You are Sophie's e-pal. Talk about yourself.
- where you're from
- your nationality
- what languages you speak

d Make up information to complete the chart. Ask and answer questions about these people.

Name	City	Country	Nationality	Language
Kenji	_____	_____	_____	_____
Nick	_____	_____	_____	_____
Julia	_____	_____	_____	_____

A: Where's Kenji from?

B: He's from Tokyo.

A: Where's that?

B: In Japan.

2 Reading

a You would like an e-pal. What do you want to know about him or her? Check ✔ the items in the first column of boxes below.

Information		Alexander's e-mail
name	☐	☐
age	☐	☐
birthday	☐	☐
city / country	☐	☐
nationality	☐	☐
interests and hobbies	☐	☐
family	☐	☐

b Read the following e-mail message. What information does Alexander provide? Check ✔ the items in the second column of boxes above.

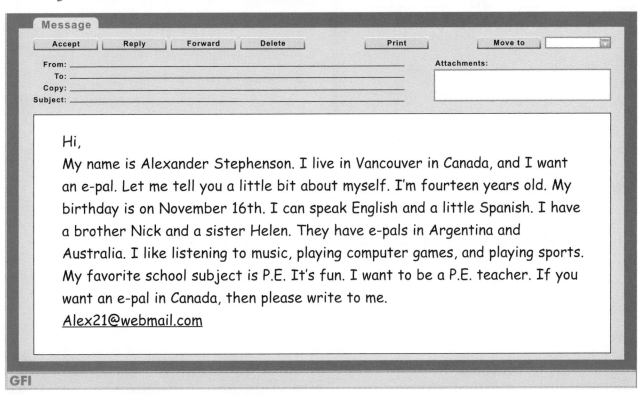

Message

| Accept | Reply | Forward | Delete | Print | Move to | ▼ |

From: _____ Attachments:
To: _____
Copy: _____
Subject: _____

Hi,

My name is Alexander Stephenson. I live in Vancouver in Canada, and I want an e-pal. Let me tell you a little bit about myself. I'm fourteen years old. My birthday is on November 16th. I can speak English and a little Spanish. I have a brother Nick and a sister Helen. They have e-pals in Argentina and Australia. I like listening to music, playing computer games, and playing sports. My favorite school subject is P.E. It's fun. I want to be a P.E. teacher. If you want an e-pal in Canada, then please write to me.

Alex21@webmail.com

GFI

c Answer these questions.

1. Where is Alexander from? _____

2. What's his nationality? _____

3. How old is he? _____

4. How many brothers and sisters does he have? _____

5. What are his hobbies? _____

3 Writing

a Complete the e-pal letter with information from the notes.

Message

PEN PAL WANTED

My name is _____
_____ . I'm _____ years
old and I'm from _____.
I speak _____ and
_____ . I have a _____
Robert and a _____ Josey.
My favorite _____ is
_____ , and I play it
every Saturday. At school, I like
_____ and _____ .
My favorite movie is
_____ . Do you
know it? It's an action movie.

Please write and tell me
about yourself.
nicha@wahu.com

GFI

Family name:

Lander

First name:

Nicholas

Age: 15

Nationality:

Australian

Family: brother Robert, sister Josey

Languages: English and French

Favorite sport: soccer

Favorite subjects: art, drama

Favorite movie: Spiderman

b Write an e-mail in your notebook to Nicholas. Tell him about yourself.

4 Go for it!

Make a list of questions
and interview three of your
classmates. Ask about the
languages they speak, their
favorite sports, movies, etc.
Then tell the rest of the
class about one of them, but
don't say his/her name. The
class will guess who it is.

Unit 14

LESSON A
What are you doing?

1 Warm up

CD2
T-30

a Match the words with the activities in the picture. Listen and check your answers.

1. doing homework   <u>d</u>

2. watching TV   ___

3. cleaning   ___

4. making dinner   ___

5. reading   ___

6. listening to a CD   ___

7. doing the laundry   ___

8. talking on the telephone   ___

9. going out   ___

10. having a snack   ___

CD2
T-31

b Listen to the two conversations. (Circle) the conversation that describes the actions in the picture.

Conversation 1

Conversation 2

 c Take turns. Talk about the picture.

A: What is Juan doing?

B: He's doing his homework. What else is he doing?

A: He's _____.

2 Listen in

a **Listen to Zack and Steve. <u>Underline</u> the correct words.**

CD2
T-32 1. Zack is doing his (math / science) homework.

2. The homework is (easy / hard).

3. Steve is watching a (talk show / movie).

4. The TV program is (interesting / boring).

5. Steve (wants / doesn't want) to see a movie.

6. Steve and Zack decide to meet at the (bus stop / mall).

b **Listen to Julia and**
CD2 **Maria. Write their names**
T-33 **on the correct pictures.**

c **Student A is Jim. Student B is Maria. Follow the instructions, and have a conversation.**

Jim	Maria
Greet Maria.	Greet Jim.
Ask Maria if she's doing her homework.	Reply. Say what you're doing.
Ask Maria what it's like.	Reply and ask Jim if he's watching TV.
Reply. Say what you're doing.	Ask Jim what it's like.
Reply.	Invite Jim to the mall.
Reply.	

3 Grammar focus

a Study the questions and answers in the chart.

Questions	Answers	
Are you doing your homework?	Yes, I am.	No, I'm not. I'm watching TV.
Is he reading?	Yes, he is.	No, he isn't. He's writing e-mails.
Are they doing the laundry?	Yes, they are.	No, they aren't. They're cleaning their bedroom.
What are you doing?	I'm making lunch.	
What are they watching?	They're watching a game show on TV.	
What is she doing?	She's doing her homework.	

Look!
What are you wearing to the party?
I'm wearing a blue sweater.

What's Jean wearing?
She's wearing a pair of jeans and a T-shirt.

b Make up questions following the example.

1. Mom cleans the house every Saturday.   Is your mom cleaning the house right now?
2. My dad makes dinner every Friday.   _____?
3. Alicia wears jeans to school every day.   _____?
4. Tom plays video games after school.   _____?
5. Martina does her homework every evening. _____?
6. Susan and Bob talk on the phone every day. _____?

c Unscramble this telephone conversation. Then practice it. Practice again using other actions from the unit.

____ I'm getting ready for the party.

____ I'm wearing a pair of jeans and a T-shirt.

____ What are you wearing?

__1__ What are you doing?

____ I'm wearing my new jeans and a sweater. How about you?

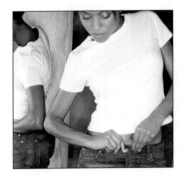

4 Get it together

Look at your classmates for two minutes, and then close your eyes. Your classmates will ask you what different people are wearing.

A: What's Alicia wearing?

B: She's wearing blue jeans.

LESSON B I'm doing my homework.

1 Talk about it

a Draw lines to match the places to the activities. Choose an activity and then have a conversation with your partner.

Internet café

gym

mall

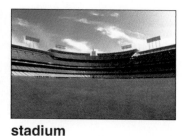
stadium

eating lunch

surfing the Web

kickboxing

watching a game

A: Where are you?

B: I'm at the mall.

A: What are you doing?

B: I'm eating lunch with a friend.

b Listen and fill in the chart.

CD2
T-34

Name	Place	Activity
Tina	_____	_____
Mike	_____	_____
Yumiko	_____	_____
Francisco	_____	_____

c Complete the chart with locations, activities, and invitations. Then practice a telephone conversation with your partner.

Location	Activity	Invitation
mall	shopping for a present	watch a soccer game
_____	_____	_____
_____	_____	_____
_____	_____	_____

2 Reading

a What sports can you play at your school? Make a list. Which ones do you like or dislike? Which ones are you good at or not good at? Check ✓ the columns.

Sport	Like?	Don't like?	Good at?	Not good at?
_____	_____	_____	_____	_____
_____	_____	_____	_____	_____
_____	_____	_____	_____	_____

b Scan Richard's home page. ⟨Circle⟩ his activities. Do you like the same sports that Richard likes? Are you good at the same things?

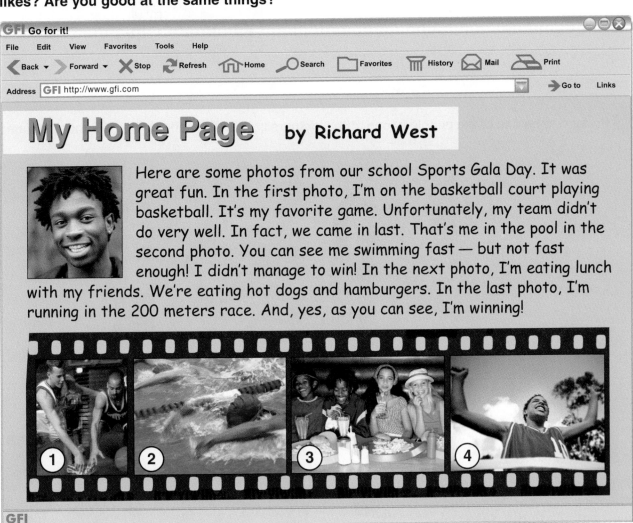

My Home Page by Richard West

Here are some photos from our school Sports Gala Day. It was great fun. In the first photo, I'm on the basketball court playing basketball. It's my favorite game. Unfortunately, my team didn't do very well. In fact, we came in last. That's me in the pool in the second photo. You can see me swimming fast — but not fast enough! I didn't manage to win! In the next photo, I'm eating lunch with my friends. We're eating hot dogs and hamburgers. In the last photo, I'm running in the 200 meters race. And, yes, as you can see, I'm winning!

c Read Richard's home page and then write captions for the photos.

1. Look at me. I'm _____.

2. Here I am. I'm _____.

3. This is me and my friends. We're _____.

4. Wow! Look at me here! I'm _____.

3 Writing

a Fill in the blanks.

Dear Bob,

Here is a photo of my family. I'm wearing a red T-shirt, and I'm doing my homework. My father and mother are _____.

My grandfather is _____.

My brother is _____.

And my big sister is _____

_____.

b Pretend to be one of the people in one of the pictures below. Write about yourself and your family.

_____

_____

_____

4 Go for it!

Play a slide show game. Take turns miming different activities. Your partner describes their actions to the class.

John is playing basketball. Michael is . . .

Language review 7

a Complete the chart.

Country	Nationality	Language
1. Brazil		
2.	American	
3.	Australian	
4. Canada		English and
5.	Mexican	
6.		Korean
7. the United Kingdom		
8.		Japanese

b Unscramble the questions. Then write the answers.

1. Taiwan What they speak in language do

_____?

_____.

2. speak they do Turkish Where

_____?

_____.

3. nationality your What's

_____?

_____.

4. your from parents are Where

_____?

_____.

c Fill in the blanks in this e-mail message.

> **Message**
>
> Hi,
> My (1)_____ is Bryan Davis. I (2)_____ in Washington,
> (4)_____ the United States. I'm fifteen (5)_____ old. My
> (6)_____ is on March 1st. I can (7)_____ English and Spanish. I
> (8)_____ two brothers, Kevin and Dewayne. I (9)_____ movies,
> computer games, and sports. My favorite (10) _____ is tennis. I want an
> e-pal, so please (11)_____ to me. Thanks!

GFI

d **Look at the picture. Write questions and answers.**

1. Dave / eat ice cream

   <u>Is Dave eating ice cream? No, he isn't. He's eating a hamburger.</u>

2. Sue / read

   _____

3. Jim and Tim / play tennis

   _____

4. Sue and Dave / listen to music

   _____

5. Jim / wear a t-shirt

   _____

Learning log

Write ten useful words you learned in
Units 13 and 14.

1. _____
2. _____
3. _____
4. _____
5. _____
6. _____
7. _____
8. _____
9. _____
10. _____

I can:	Yes	Need more practice
talk about countries and languages	☐	☐
ask questions with **where**	☐	☐
talk about what people are doing	☐	☐
start a telephone conversation	☐	☐

Unit 15

LESSON A
Where's the food court?

1 Warm up

CD2 T-35

a Match the words with the places in the picture. Listen and check your answers.

1. food court   _h_

2. bookstore   ___

3. hair salon   ___

4. video arcade   ___

5. gym   ___

6. ATM   ___

7. movie theater   ___

8. pet shop   ___

9. sports store   ___

10. computer store ___

CD2 T-36

b Listen and (circle) the places you hear.

food court

video arcade

ATM

sports store

bookstore

movie theater

Where's the food court?

It's next to the movie theater.

 C Practice the conversation. Then talk about other places in the picture.

A: Excuse me.

B: Yes?

A: Is there an ATM near here?

B: Yes. There's one next to the pet shop.

2 Listen in

a Match the sentences and the pictures.
CD2 Listen and check ✓ the sentences you
T-37 hear.

____ 1. The ATM is across from the pet shop.

____ 2. The ATM is on the second floor.

____ 3. The ATM is between the sports store
and the gym.

____ 4. The ATM is next to the bookstore.

b Listen and check ✓ the things Michael
CD2 wants to find.
T-38

____ video arcade

____ food court

____ gym

____ movie theater

____ bookstore

____ hair salon

____ computer store

____ ATM

c Listen and mark these places
CD2 with letters on the map.
T-39

C = computer store

B = bookstore

P = pet shop

A = ATM

d Ask and answer questions about where
places are located in the mall.

A: Where is the gym?

B: It's next to the sports store.

3 Grammar focus

a Study the questions and answers in the chart.

Questions	Answers
Where's the sports store?	It's across from the gym.
Where's the pet shop?	It's on the second floor.
Where's the movie theater?	It's between the video arcade and the food court.
Where are the ATMs?	They're next to the food court.

b Order these words to make sentences.

LOOK!

Is there a gym around here?

Yes. There's a gym on the second floor.

Are there any ATMs near here?

Yes. There's one at the mall.

1. The is between sports store and the video arcade the hair salon

_____

2. on pet shop is The floor second the

_____

3. ATMs next to The are bookstore the

_____

4. movie theater is The across from computer the store

_____

5. next to video arcade The is sports store the

_____

c Make up five statements and five questions from these words. Practice the conversations.

the ATMs here near is any are there a on movie theater where bookstore second floor they're next to it's food court and between

Is there a bookstore near here?

4 Get it together

Play a game with two teams. Think of a place in your neighborhood. Don't say the name of the place. Students from the other team ask questions to guess the place.

Is it near the gym?

No, it isn't.

LESSON B Is there a park in your neighborhood?

1 Talk about it

a Match the words with things in the picture.

<u>a</u> park

___ supermarket

___ basketball court

___ newsstand

___ apartment building

___ bakery

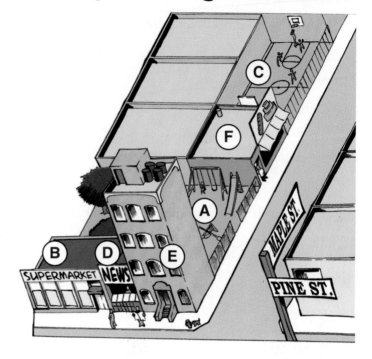

b Listen and (circle) the places in the picture that you hear mentioned. Then write answers to the questions and practice the conversations.

CD2
T-40

A: Is there a newsstand in the neighborhood?

B: Yes. It's on Pine Street.

① Where's the park?

② Where's the supermarket?

③ Is there a bakery in the neighborhood?

big   small

quiet   noisy

C Ask your partner about where he or she lives.

A: Is there a big supermarket where you live?   B: Yes, there is.

 2 Reading

a You are going to read about Amelia's neighborhood. She says it's the perfect neighborhood. Can you predict what she writes?

___ There's a big video arcade next door.

___ The street is very busy.

___ There's a quiet park nearby.

___ The street is very quiet.

___ There's a big supermarket nearby.

___ My school is close to my house.

___ My house is next to a big hotel.

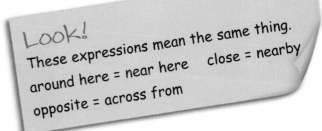

LOOK!
These expressions mean the same thing.
around here = near here   close = nearby
opposite = across from

 b Now read about Amelia's neighborhood and check your predictions.

Last month we had a competition to find the perfect neighborhood. This month we publish the winning entry by Amelia Stranks from Class 9C. Congratulations, Amelia!

My Perfect Neighborhood

BY AMELIA STRANKS

I live in the perfect neighborhood. The street is very quiet. Some people like lots of noise and crowds, but I like my quiet street. My house is between a big park and an apartment building. On the weekend, I sometimes buy a magazine from the newsstand and sit in the park to read it. There is a big supermarket not too far away. Next to the supermarket is a small basketball court.

Across the street is a bakery, and next to the bakery is a video store where I can rent videos. So, you see, my neighborhood has everything I need. The only thing that isn't close is my school. In fact, I need to take two buses to get to school.

c Read the article again. Write **T** for true, **F** for false and **?** for "don't know."

___ 1. Amelia won a competition.

___ 2. She lives on a busy street.

___ 3. Her house is opposite a supermarket.

___ 4. She buys a magazine on weekends.

___ 5. She sometimes rents videos.

___ 6. She has a long way to travel to school.

3 Writing

a Look at the picture, and fill in the blanks in the following passage. Use these words.

between
big
noisy
quiet
small
video arcade

I live on Bridge Street. It's a very _____ noisy _____ street. There is a _____

supermarket on the corner. Next to the supermarket is a _____ library and a big

_____ . _____ the bakery and the video arcade is a _____ park.

b Write about your own neighborhood.

4 Go for it!

Talk about the perfect neighborhood.
Then take turns drawing a map of
your perfect neighborhood. Present
your neighborhood to the rest of
the class.

Unit 16

LESSON A
Why do you like snakes?

1 Warm up

CD2
T-41

a Match the words with the pictures. Listen and check your answers.

1. cat   _b_
2. dog   ___
3. spider   ___
4. rat   ___
5. snake   ___
6. hamster   ___
7. ant farm   ___
8. parrot   ___
9. ferret   ___
10. turtle   ___

CD2
T-42

b Listen and (circle) the words you hear.

parrot	dog
ant farm	spider
snake	hamster
rat	

Let's get Jane a dog for her birthday.

She doesn't like dogs.

Why doesn't she like dogs?

Because they're noisy.

C Practice the conversation. Then make up conversations about other animals in the picture. Use words you know.

scary   noisy   fun   interesting   small

A: Let's get a spider.

B: Why do you like spiders?

A: Because I think they're kind of scary.

2 Listen in

a Listen to the conversation. Put the sentences in the correct order.

CD2
T-43

___ I can't have a dog.

___ Then get a turtle. They're small and quiet.

___ Why?

__1__ Let's look at the dogs.

___ Because they're big and noisy.

b Listen and (circle) the animals that Lucy and Sam discuss.

CD2
T-44

c Listen again and check ✓ the animals that Lucy and Sam like. Put an X next to the animals they don't like. Write a ? for "I don't know."

CD2
T-45

Lucy	Sam
___ ant farms	___ ant farms
___ cats	___ cats
___ dogs	___ dogs
___ spiders	___ spiders
___ snakes	___ snakes
___ hamsters	___ hamsters
___ ferrets	___ ferrets

d Practice the conversation.

A: Why does Lucy like _____?

B: Because, they're _____.

A: Why doesn't she like the _____?

B: Because it's _____.

3 Grammar focus

 Study the questions and answers in the chart.

Questions	Answers
Why do you like this dog?	Because it's very cool.
Why does Sam like snakes?	Because they're really interesting.
Why do they want a cat?	Because they're fun.

> **LOOK!**
> Where do they come in the sentence?
> It's **really** fun.
> These dogs are **very** cool.
> It's **kind of** scary.

b Write the words in the correct spaces. Then practice the conversation.

because	do	don't	cool	like	Why

A: Do you _____ rats?

B: No, I _____ . I'm scared of them. But I like spiders.

A: Really? _____ do you like spiders?

B: Well, _____ they're kind of interesting. Do you like spiders?

A: Yes, I guess. I like snakes a lot.

B: Snakes? You're kidding! Why _____ you like snakes?

A: They're really _____ .

c Write the names of animals in the blanks to make statements that are true for you.

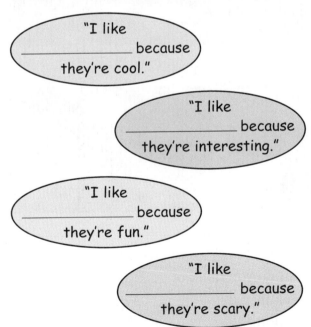

"I like _____ because they're cool."

"I like _____ because they're interesting."

"I like _____ because they're fun."

"I like _____ because they're scary."

4 Get it together

Select nine words from the list and write each one in one of the squares below. your teacher will call out the words. Listen and cross out (X) the words you hear. Say **Bingo!** when you get a row of Xs. The first person to get a row of Xs in any direction is the winner.

dog	cat	spider	rat	snake
hamster	ant farm	parrot	rabbit	turtle
interesting	exciting	fun	cool	scary

LESSON B I think dolphins are friendly.

1 Talk about it

a Read the words that describe the pictures.

friendly   intelligent   shy   beautiful

Animals

dangerous   fast

b Listen and look at the pictures. (Circle) the animals that Maria says are endangered.

CD2
T-46

tiger

dangerous

panda

shark

dolphin

gorilla

eagle

c Write a word from below each animal. You can use a word more than once. Then talk about the animals with other students.

A: What do you think of _____?
B: I think they're _____. What do you think?
A: I think they're _____.

2 Reading

a What do you think? Check ✔ the animals you think are endangered.

Dolphins ☐	Tigers ☐
Pandas ☐	Gorillas ☐
Koalas ☐	Eagles ☐

b Read the article quickly, and decide on the best name for the Web site.

___ Do you know what a panda is?   ___ Visit San Diego Zoo

___ Blackwood High "Save the Panda" Project   ___ Pandas make great pets.

GFI Go for it!

File   Edit   View   Favorites   Tools   Help

Back ▾   Forward ▾   ✕ Stop   ⟳ Refresh   ⌂ Home   🔍 Search   🗀 Favorites   History   ✉ Mail   Print

Address GFI   ➜ Go to   Links

Hello. We are students at Blackwood High, and this is our Web site. We have a project to help save pandas. We want to make people aware that these creatures are in great danger.

Pandas are cute, black-and-white bears that live in central China. Although they are intelligent, they are also very shy. Everyone knows what a panda looks like, but very few people have ever seen one in real life. This is because they are very rare. There are only about 1,000 pandas left that live in the forests of central China. Another 120 pandas live in zoos in China. About 20 more live in zoos in other countries.

Would you like to see a panda? The San Diego Zoo in California has a webcam in its panda house. You can visit the zoo's Web site and watch the pandas.

GFI

---

c Read the article again and answer these questions.

1. What is the purpose of the Blackwood High project?

_____

2. What is a word in the passage that has the same meaning as "animal"?

_____

3. Are pandas dangerous? _____

4. What three words do the students use to describe pandas?

_____

5. How many pandas are there in the world? _____

---

3 Writing

a Put these sentences in order to make a paragraph.

_____ Because they're intelligent and friendly.

_____ Nellie is a twelve-year-old female elephant from Africa.

_____ Why don't you come and visit her this weekend?

_____ Why do I like elephants?

_____ They're also very big, as you can see from this photo of Nellie.

_____ She is the most popular creature at Blackwood Zoo.

_____ My favorite animals are elephants.

__1__ Hi, my name is Rita Merrony and I'm a keeper at Blackwood Zoo.

Visit the Blackwood Zoo.

Z
O
O

Z
O
O

b Imagine that you are a zookeeper. Write your own brochure about a different zoo animal.

4 Go for it!

One student is an animal expert; other students are visitors to the zoo. The animal expert gives information about an animal. Visitors ask questions.

Are dolphins dangerous?

Language review 8

a Look at the map and complete the sentences.

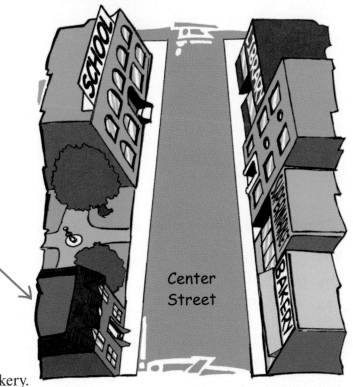

My house

Center Street

1. I live _____ Center Street.

2. My house is _____ the bakery.

3. There's a big park _____.

4. My school is _____ the park.

5. The supermarket is _____ the bakery and the apartment building.

6. The apartment building is _____ the school.

b Unscramble the places.

1. soph ept   _____
2. odive raceda _____
3. psrost serot _____
4. pmocture ersto _____
5. arih lnoas   _____
6. besokorot   _____

c Ask questions with **Is there** or **Are there**.

1. busy streets / your city   <u>Are there any busy streets in your city?</u>
2. supermarket / your neighborhood _____
3. parks / your town   _____
4. bookstore / near here   _____
5. movie theater / your school   _____
6. bakery / this street   _____
7. computer store / your city   _____

d Write lists of animals under the descriptive words. Use your own opinion.

interesting	fun	noisy
_____	_____	_____
_____	_____	_____
_____	_____	_____

cute	scary	small
_____	_____	_____
_____	_____	_____
_____	_____	_____

e Complete the conversations about animals.

1. You: Let's get a _____ .

    Your friend: Why _____ ?

    You: Because _____ .

2. Your friend: Do you like _____ ?

    You: No, _____ . They're _____ . But I like _____ .

    Your friend: Really? Why _____ ?

    You: I think _____ .

3. You: What do you think _____ ?

    Your friend: I _____ . What _____ ?

    You: _____ .

Learning log

Write ten useful words you learned in Units 15 and 16.

1. _____
2. _____
3. _____
4. _____
5. _____
6. _____
7. _____
8. _____
9. _____
10. _____

I can:	Yes	Need more practice
talk about places in my town	☐	☐
ask questions about places	☐	☐
talk about animals	☐	☐
give reasons with **because**	☐	☐

Contents

Make your own Web page!

Use three photos or drawings:

Picture #1: you

Write your first name, last name, and phone number.

Picture #2: your family

Write about your family.

Picture #3: your room

Write about your room.

My Web page

Hi!
My first name is Katie.
My last name is Ramos.
My phone number is 555-1212.

This is my family.
These are my parents.
This is my sister, Lily.

This is my room.
My books are on my desk.
My dog is under my bed!

Write for your class newspaper!

Interview a classmate. Ask questions about his or her . . .

hobbies: _____

favorite sports: _____

favorite foods: _____

favorite colors: _____

Then write an article for your class newspaper and draw pictures.

All about Rafael

Rafael Torres is a student in English 202. His favorite color is red.

His hobbies are computer games and music. He collects CDs.

His favorite sport is baseball, and his favorite player is Sammy Sosa. He also likes basketball. He doesn't like soccer.

His favorite food is dessert! He likes ice cream, cake, chocolate, and fruit. He doesn't like fish.

Project 3

Do a class survey!

Choose a topic.

colors
sports
hobbies
school subjects
food
movies

Think of a question

What's your favorite kind of movie?

Ask your classmates. Write their answers.

Name	Favorite kind of movie	Name	Favorite kind of movie
Celia	comedy		
Takashi	action		
Jose Luis	comedy		
Sun-Hee	drama		

Put the answers together and make a poster.

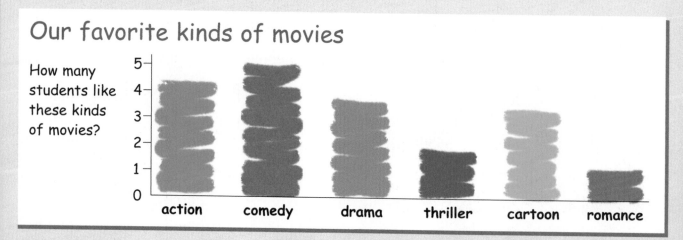

Our favorite kinds of movies

How many students like these kinds of movies?

Project 4

Write a city guide!

Choose a famous place in your city. Get information about the place.

Where is it? _____

What's it like? _____

What can you do there? _____

Then write a guidebook page and draw pictures.

Center Park

It's close to our school. It's on the corner of Park Street and Lake Street.

It's very quiet and beautiful. There are big trees and many flowers.

You can meet your friends and have a picnic. You can play tennis and volleyball. It's fun!

Student A
Communicative activity 1

Finish the picture!
Student A and Student B have different pictures.
Ask questions to finish your picture.

Draw: pencil case, keys, baseball cap,
       sunglasses, telephone
Write: name and telephone number.

Now look at your pictures. Are they the same?

Communicative activity 2

Crossword puzzle
Talk to your partner to finish this puzzle.
You have the "Across" clues, and your
partner has the "Down" clues.

Across

2. Let's ___ baseball.

3. How ___ is that swimsuit?

5. Apples and oranges are ___.

6. The color of bananas is ___.

7. Spell 18.

10. I eat ___ in the morning.

11. The color of broccoli is ___.

13. Month #12 is ___.

14. Is your ___ in September?

16. Spell 40.

17. Tomatoes and broccoli are ___.

Student A

Communicative activity 3

The schedule game

You want to see a movie with your partner on Saturday. Here is your schedule and a movie schedule. Your partner has different schedules. Talk to your partner and choose a movie.

Useful sentences:
Are you busy at 8:00?
What kind of movie is it?
What time is that movie?
Let's see _____ .

SATURDAY

9:00-11:00	Study in the library
1:00-2:00	Computer class

Cinema Club

"September Love"	(romantic)	1:30, 4:15, 7:45, 10:00
"Terminator 15"	(action)	5:45, 8:15, 11:00
"Baby Animals"	(documentary)	1:45, 3:45, 5:45
"Queen Elizabeth"	(historical drama)	3:00, 5:30, 8:15, 11:30

Communicative activity 4

Different pictures

Talk to your partner. What's different in your partner's picture? (Circle) ten things.

Student B
Communicative activity 1

Finish the picture!
Student A and Student B have different pictures.
Ask questions to finish your picture.

Where's the ID card?

It's on the table.

Draw: ruler, notebook, TV,
    alarm clock, comics
Write: name and telephone number.

Now look at your pictures. Are they the same?

Communicative activity 2

Crossword puzzle
Talk to your partner to finish this puzzle.
You have the "Down" clues, and your
partner has the "Across" clues.

Down

1. Month #1 is ____.
4. I ____ soccer cards.
5. Spell 15.
8. It's not boring. It's ____.
9. The color of apples is ____.
12. Do you have a tennis ____?
15. ____ Ali like hamburgers?

Student B
Communicative activity 3

The schedule game
You want to see a movie with your partner on Saturday. Here is your schedule and a movie schedule. Your partner has different schedules. Talk to your partner and choose a movie.

Useful sentences:
Are you busy at 8:00?
What kind of movie is it?
What time is that movie?
Let's see _____ .

SATURDAY

9:00-12:00   Soccer practice

6:00   Dinner with Grandmother

Movie Town

"Two Mothers, One Child"	(drama)	2:00, 4:30, 8:00, 10:15
"Race Against Time"	(thriller)	5:15, 7:00, 8:45, 10:30
"Motor Mouse Festival"	(cartoon)	4:00, 7:30, 10:00
"Our House"	(comedy)	3:15, 5:15, 7:15, 9:15

Communicative activity 4

Different pictures
Talk to your partner. What's different in your partner's picture? (Circle) ten things.

Language Summary

Unit 1 New friends
Expressions: My name's Gina.
What's your phone number?

Present tense: *to be*

I'm = I am	Mary.
He's = He is	Kenji.
She's = She is	Anna.
We're = We are	Tony and Greg.
They're = They are	

What questions

What's	your	name? phone number?

Possessive adjectives

My Your His Her	name is	Rosa. Tom. David. Maria.

Unit 2 My things
Expressions: That's my ruler.
How do you spell backpack?

Demonstratives

This ↓ o	That →→→→→o	
This is That's = That is	my his your	backpack. book. ruler.

Yes/No questions and short answers

Is	this that	my your his her	pencil? book? watch? wallet?	Yes, it is. No, it isn't.

Unit 3 Family
Expressions: Nice to meet you.
This is my family/sister/brother.

Subject pronouns

| I |
| you |
| he |
| she |
| they |

Plural nouns

Singular = 1	Plural > 1
one brother one sister one cousin	two brothers three sisters ten cousins

Unit 4 At home

Expressions: Where is my backpack?
Is my math book on the bed?

Where questions

Where's	my	baseball? backpack?
Where are	my	books? keys?

Prepositions: *on, in, under*

	under	the box.	
It's	in	the box.	
	on	the box.	

Unit 5 Free time

Expressions: Do you have a soccer ball?
Let's play computer games!

Present tense: *to have*

I You We They	have	a tennis racket. a baseball. a skateboard.
He She	has	

Let's

Let's	watch a video. play basketball. read comic books.

Do/Don't, Does/Doesn't

Do	you we they	have	a baseball?	Yes,	I we they	do.	No,	I we they	don't.
Does	he she				he she	does.		he she	doesn't.

Unit 6 Food

Expressions: Do you like bananas?
I like some fruit, but I hate bananas!

Present tense: *to like*

I You We They	like	ice cream. chicken. apples.
He She	likes	

Negative statements

I You We They	don't	like	fish. hamburgers. pizza.
He She	doesn't		

Unit 7 Shopping

Expressions: How much are these pants?
The shorts are sixteen dollars.

How much

How much	is	that shirt? this bag?	It's twenty dollars. It's eight dollars.
	are	these pants? these jeans?	They're fifteen dollars. They're thirty dollars.

Reference word: *one*

I like the blue cap. I want the black shorts.	= I like the blue one. = I want the black ones.

Unit 8 Special days

Expressions: My birthday's in November.
When is the class party?

When questions / Prepositions of time: in, *on*

When	is	your birthday? the English test? our party? the baseball game?	It's	in	April. September.
				on	July 1st. August 5th.

Possessive: *-'s*

Mark's Leila's My sister's	birthday party	is	on Monday.

Unit 9 Videos

Expressions: Do you want to rent a video?
Thrillers are scary.

And / But

✓ I like ✓ I play ✓ I have	thrillers, tennis, a baseball,	and	✓ I like ✓ I play ✓ I have	action movies. basketball. a skateboard.
✓ I like ✓ I play ✓ I have	comedies, soccer, a baseball,	but	✗ I don't like ✗ I don't play ✗ I don't have	cartoons. volleyball. a bat.

Present tense: *to want*

I We You They	want	to	watch videos. read comic books. eat lunch.
He She	wants		

Plural: *-s, -ies*

Singular = 1	Plural > 1
one thriller one cartoon	two thrillers three cartoons
one comedy one documentary	ten comedies four documentaries

Unit 10 Know-how

Expressions: Can you play the guitar?
Bill can play the guitar, but he can't sing.

Can (ability)

I You He We They Maria	can can't	play tennis. sing. speak English.

Can	you John they	speak Spanish? play soccer? cook?

Unit 11 Daily routines

Expressions: What time do you usually go to school?
When do you exercise?

What time questions/ Preposition of time: *at*

What time When	do you does he do they	go to bed? get up? eat lunch?	At 11:00. At 6:30. At 1:00.

Adverbs of frequency

I We	always usually sometimes	get up at 7:00.

Unit 12 School subjects

Expressions: My favorite subject is science.
Music is cool.

Why questions / *Because*

Why	do you do you does she	like science? hate P.E.? like math?	Because	it's fun. it's boring. it's interesting.

Who questions

Who is Who's	your	science teacher? friend?

Unit 13 Around the world

Expressions: Where is your e-pal from?
What languages do you speak?

Where questions with *from* and *live*

Where	are you are they is he	from?	I'm They're He's	from	Canada.
	do you do they does he	live?	I They	live	in Toronto.
			He	lives	

Unit 14 Everyday activities
Expressions: What are you doing?
I'm doing my homework.

Present progressive

I'm	watching TV.
You're	eating ice cream.
He's	shopping.
She's	playing tennis.
We're	doing homework.
They're	reading.

Yes/No questions

Am I	
Are you	
Is he	shopping?
Is she	playing soccer?
Are we	reading?
Are they	

What questions

What	are you	doing?
	is he	watching?
	are they	reading?

Unit 15 Around town
Expressions: Where's the food court?
Is there a park in your neighborhood?

Prepositions of place: *between, across from, next to*

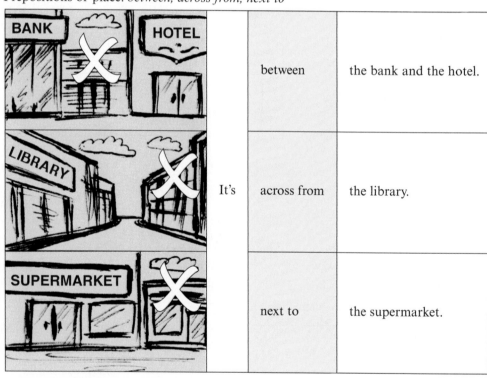

	between	the bank and the hotel.
It's	across from	the library.
	next to	the supermarket.

Unit 16 Animals
Expressions: Why do you like snakes?
I think dolphins are friendly.

Why questions / *Because*

Why	do you	like dogs?	Because	they're intelligent.
	don't you	like snakes?		they're scary.
	does he	play tennis?		it's fun.
	doesn't she	drink soda?		it's unhealthy.

Adverbs: *very, really, kind of*

I think spiders are	kind of really very	scary.

Vocabulary Index

Skills Index

Around the world U13
Around town U15
Daily routines U11
Everyday activities U14
Family U3
Food U6
Free time U5
Friends U1
Home U4
Personal belongings U2
School subjects U12
Shopping U7
Special days U8
Videos U9

Viewing
Respond to a visual image U1, U2, U3, U4, U5, U6, U7, U8, U9, U10, U11, U12, U13, U14, U15, U16

Vocabulary
Action verbs U10, U11, U14
Adjectives of quality U5, U9, U12, U16
Alphabet U2
Animals U16
Clothes U7
Colors U7
Collocations
Countries U13
Days of the week U12
Events U8
Family members U3
Food U6

Furniture U4
Greetings U1
Habitats U16
Languages U13
Locations U14
Meals U6
Months U8
Musical instruments U10
Nationalities U13
Numbers 0-9 U1
Numbers 10-31
Ordinals 1-31 U8
Personal belongings U2
Places U15
Rooms of the house U4
School subjects U12
Sports objects U5
Time U11
Video genres U9

Writing
I.D. card U1
Messages U2, U4
Letters U3
Survey U5
Description U6, U11, U12, U14, U15
Advertisement U7
Article for school newspaper U8
Movie review U9
Application U10
E-mail U13
Brochure U16